# Enchanted Evening Barbie and the Second Coming

ALSO BY RHETA GRIMSLEY JOHNSON

*America's Faces* (1987)

*Good Grief: The Story of Charles M. Schulz* (1989)

*Poor Man's Provence: Finding Myself in Cajun Louisiana* (2008)

# Enchanted Evening Barbie and the Second Coming

a memoir by

## RHETA GRIMSLEY JOHNSON

NEWSOUTH BOOKS
Montgomery | Louisville

NewSouth Books
105 S. Court Street
Montgomery, AL 36104

Library of Congress Cataloging-in-Publication Data

Johnson, Rheta Grimsley, 1953-
Enchanted evening Barbie and the second coming : a memoir /
by Rheta Grimsley Johnson.

p. cm.

ISBN-13: 978-1-58838-250-4
ISBN-10: 1-58838-250-8

1. Johnson, Rheta Grimsley, 1953- 2. Journalists—United States—Biography.
I. Title.
PN4874.J585A3 2010
070.92—dc22
[B]

2010002123

Design by Randall Williams

Printed in the United States of America
by Thomson-Shore, Inc.

For my refrigerator babies, Chelsey and Ben

And for Don

# CONTENTS

# Acknowledgments

In January 2009, I started writing a book, a Christmas book, a humorous book, one that chronicled my professional and personal life by remembering pivotal holidays. The idea seemed a bit contrived, but I needed to write a book that would sell, and Christmas books, funny books, generally do.

I had written precious few words by the time of Don's unexpected death in March. For weeks I pretty much abandoned the project, feeling too cheerless to tackle a book on any subject, much less Christmas.

Then, one day, whether by habit or in desperation or in an attempt at self-medication, I started writing again. It was a Christmas book, but it was more. Christmas became a skeleton, a minor theme, a string tying together a bigger bundle. Writing is always hard, but at times it can be *necessary*, too. It was necessary for me to write this book and to write it this way. And it was hard.

Friends helped. Sue and Luke Hall fed me. Terry Martin and Anne Holtsford and Anita McRae and Bobbie Williams and Barbara Sweeney, all of them cheered me on though they mostly had no idea what I was writing. Johnelle and Jeanette took care of Henderson business so I could stay home and write. Tom and Jennifer Fox read a rough draft. Jimmy encouraged me, as he always does. Annie Bates, dealing with her own grief over Don's death, gave of herself at every turn. Annie and I got through the days in a duet of tight harmony and deep sadness.

NewSouth's Randall Williams and Suzanne La Rosa gave me money, extra time, moral support, and direction. I am forever and sincerely grateful to both of them.

I don't know what Don would say or think about this book, if the dead were capable of rendering judgment. They are not. I think he'd at least be proud that I finished it.

— R. G. J.

Enchanted Evening Barbie
and the Second Coming

# Rapture on Hold

M other was a woman possessed in the weeks leading up to Christmas. She made candles, using Foremost milk cartons, paraffin from a box, and Number Two yellow pencils with string wound around them to suspend the wicks. She baked. She cleaned. We cleaned at her behest. Every room in the house, including the bathroom, had what she lovingly called "a touch of Christmas."

The boxes came down from the attic, each labeled with what amounted to a cryptic description of Christmas: *Better, store-bought items and music boxes. Nutcrackers and nativity. Candles with glitter. Santa Claus bank and table-toppers. Angel with rhinestones.*

Her enthusiasm was infectious. For weeks I would lie sleepless on the black iron bed—hospital beds they are called—looking up at the blue electric candles in their plastic candelabra that glowed through the curtains in my window. A good little Baptist, I believed the Second Coming was imminent, as sure as spring crabgrass, that is, if Jesus didn't return before spring. And though secretly I never was comfortable with the idea of rising up from this world that I knew and loved, it was clear from the Southern Baptist sermons that we were supposed to rejoice in this idea of going on up to Glory to be with the rest of the saints. So my prayers before Christmas covered all bases and were carefully self-edited, honest in the way you are only if you think someone's looking, careful to make it clear I looked forward to the Rapture, but also getting a plug in for my preferred timetable for Jesus's return.

"Dear God," I'd begin, squeezing my eyes against the aqua electric candlelight burning in the window of our little subdivision house in Montgomery, Alabama. I had been trained to talk to God with my eyes closed, head bowed. It was the only sincere way.

"I look forward to the return of your Only Son Jesus. But could you please wait until after Christmas because I really, really, really want an Enchanted Evening Barbie dress for my Barbie doll? But I will be happy with whatever Santa brings me. Thank you and good night. Amen."

Another year I asked for a delay of the Almighty's endgame until after I got my Visible Horse, the one equine model I didn't have that showed all the bones and guts of a horse through its clear plastic skin, a must-have for the girl who seriously wanted to become a veterinarian. And I didn't know a single girl from eight to ten who didn't want to be a veterinarian. Never mind I had the wrong side of the brain for math and science. I would make up for those mental deficits with a petting hand that wouldn't stop and a big heart. Why I had a year's worth of *Appaloosa Magazine* under my bed, the pages dog-eared at photos of that spotted champion Joker B. I was halfway there.

I'VE DECIDED THAT MY Christmas prayer that particular year might have been the only time the Almighty got a message that included a reference to the Visible Horse. At any rate, God obliged. Christmas came and went, came and went, year after year, and the Perfect Man whose birthday it celebrated never once appeared for the party. Thank goodness. For Christmas was far too wonderful to confuse with its Christian origins, too much about the fun of decorating and eating and Santa Claus to entertain a downer like corpses floating up, loosed somehow from concrete vaults, to convene in the sky. That would be better drama, say, at Halloween.

So Mother kept making candles, and for a long while I kept believing in Santa Claus and Jesus, even after third grade when just before Christmas I found my younger sister Sheila's tricycle carelessly and ineffectively hidden in the living room coat closet where, admittedly, few ever dared.

A family meeting was called.

"The parents sometimes have to help Santa with the larger items, things like bicycles and puppy dogs," Mother said with Daddy as her witness. I silently, mentally added "horse" to that list.

I bought it. For another two years—until a friend, who hadn't had proper upbringing, convinced me that there really wasn't an all-knowing, all-benevolent, all-forgiving man in a white beard riding around in the sky on Christmas Eve. I thus gave up most beliefs in the supernatural at the same time, hiding, for a time, the fact that I'd lost my faith in both Santa *and* God. I didn't figure one could exist if the other was a well-orchestrated fraud.

Turns out, it's perfectly okay, even healthy, to quit believing in Santa Claus. He is, after all, a fictional invention with historical heft only because of reams of literature and art and the abstract hope that there's something more magical to life than meets the eye. It's not so okay, not in these united states, to drop your belief in a god. It gives you instant pariah status, putting you in a despised minority of heretics, misfits, and eccentrics.

When you are young, and Southern, and baptized Southern Baptist, you learn ways to hide your disbelief. I had, in my youth, the all-time best disguise. I hid my budding agnosticism by going to church every time the doors opened. Church was my social life, my chance to dress up, to sing the alto in a tight harmony, to meet boys. There were Halloween hootenannies and Valentine banquets and all manner of choir tours and road trips. The Baptist road trips were where I first learned the facts of life and first saw heavy petting, which the church vehemently preached against. I saw the deacon's son get to Second Base with the preacher's daughter on the road between DeSoto State Park and Franklin, Tennessee, and that moment of choir tour voyeurism remains one of the sexiest moments in my life, though experienced from six seats away. Most of us were enthusiastically singing "I'll Walk With God"—a favorite from our tour repertoire—while the popular couple groped one another in one of the dark back seats. It had all the titillating aspects of forbidden action in a sanctimonious setting.

No bus runs as hot as a church bus.

So what wasn't to like about superficial religion? There was no lie detector test for faith. You went through the motions, kept your mouth shut, and learned to speak euphemistically. And in all honesty, I kept thinking that if I mouthed the words enough, someday I might believe again.

I knew for sure that I was perpetuating a fraud—that I truly did not believe in life after death, much less a literal Heaven and Hell and all the rest—the day our Vacation Bible School teacher, a former missionary to China who had put her tithe where her mouth was, explained believing in the Unseen this way:

"When you sit down in a chair, you don't first turn around to see if the chair is there. You simply sit," she said, demonstrating with a choir loft chair.

"Maybe *you* don't look," I thought but did not say aloud. "But if your mother had rearranged furniture as much as mine, you'd damn sure look first."

I probably didn't think "damn" at the time—my cursing facility would come later after decades in newsrooms and hanging around other newspaper reprobates—but you get the point. I still check out a chair before I sit, and that probably has saved me all kinds of embarrassment.

Later, when I left my childhood home and was able to have a social life not sanctioned by Southern Baptists, I still fudged on the belief issue. I might declare I was against "organized religion," which I was, but I never volunteered that it went much deeper. I never stopped conversation in the dormitory rooms, for instance, by interrupting my super-religious suitemate—she spent every free hour of her weekends at the Baptist Youth Union—to debate the very existence of a Supreme Being. I'm not sure anyone would have known what I was talking about. Blind acceptance was so much a part of my culture, American culture, especially Southern culture, that you'd have to have had a masochistic streak to volunteer your maverick belief, or lack of belief.

I was, in a word, a hypocrite, same as those politicians who campaign on some sanctimonious platform of family values while diddling their interns. I suspect the pious Republicans and I aren't the only hypocrites abroad in the land, but I can't know for sure. I can only know my own heart. And I refuse to pretend.

Somehow, despite my inability to embrace the supernatural, I never quite quit loving Christmas, even when I married a wise man who claimed to despise the holiday because of its tendency to aggravate depression and because of its overwrought excesses. Didn't matter. Nobody could talk me into giving up on Christmas.

Every year I still cut a tree and haul around boxes of sentimental decorations and weep over certain ornaments and get chill bumps when Willie Nelson sings "Pretty Paper." I see no reason to deny myself participation in the sport of Christmas, which has become so commercial and secularized that many nonbelievers feel quite comfortable wishing our friends a merry one, making ambrosia, and going completely over the top with decorations.

After all, I am my mother's daughter.

# 2

# Ted and the Foot-Washing Baptists

The first fuzzy Christmas memory I have involved a teddy bear, and I was three. Children today have L. L. Bean beds and hammocks piled high with an ark's worth of stuffed animals, designer tags in their ears, and most of them ignored. That wasn't the case in 1956. Santa brought one. My first.

I can remember the new smell of that bear even today, and that he had a red felt tongue that wasn't completely stitched down, the better to make him stick it out at other cars as we drove three hours on two-lane roads to get to my grandmother's south Georgia house by dark on Christmas day. In an embarrassing lapse of imagination, I named the teddy bear Ted, and for years I slept with him every night and dragged him around dirt roads and store aisles like a feather boa. I thought he could hear and understand me, which wasn't much of a leap since I believed he'd been brought by a fat man riding through the Florida sky in a sled pulled by eight tiny reindeer. Ted remains the most understanding male I've ever slept with.

We lived at the time in Pensacola, Florida, in a cinderblock house painted shell-innards pink, which was such a wonderful thing that I assumed we were rich. Poor people, I figured, did not live in pink houses, especially within walking distance of the Pensacola Bay. Daddy worked as a meat market manager, ipso facto a butcher, for the Kwik-Chek grocery store, and mother, as was conventional in the 1950s, stayed home with me and my older sister. JoAnne and I loved Pensacola, figuring the fact that we lived in sunny, celebrated Florida put us light years ahead of our country cousins back in the peanut fields of Georgia. Relatives and friends wanted to visit us, after all, to go to the sand spit called Santa Rosa Island and build sand castles along the sugar beaches and wade in the bottle-green ocean. Nobody vacationed in the crop rows of south Georgia. Nobody made postcards of peanut fields.

I believe that when you are a young child color affects your senses about as much as anything, with the possible exception of taste. Colors are what I remember best about Pensacola, where I only lived from ages one to six. Besides the pig pink house and the green water and the blinding white sand, I easily remember the rose-tinted mortar between the stones of the patio, which my father built himself, and the bold gold flowers on the drapes that Mother cherished. I remember the colored lights called "The Dancing Fountains" that played on a downtown water show set to music, and the whiskey-colored mahogany of my father's skiff on a trailer parked in our corner lot of a yard. The colors of Panhandle Florida are like a kaleidoscope I've kept in a drawer all these years. I can mix them into different patterns whenever I hold the kaleidoscope to the light.

Even our Christmas trees were pastels, sprayed with flocking in sky blue or pink, never needing many decorations, which was good because we didn't yet own many. Mother taped the Christmas cards we received to the jalousie window behind the tree. She did her best to deck the halls, but the Pensacola dwelling was more of a summer house than a Christmas one. That's the only trouble with houses in coastal towns. They need a lot of help at Christmas.

As wonderful as our patch of Florida was, it wasn't where we spent Christmas, at least not all of it. It would have been far too sane to stay put. After a quick survey of the Santa loot that was placed unwrapped beneath the tabletop tree, JoAnne and I were snatched up in our pajamas and marched to the driveway. We were allowed to pack one toy each in the car that was inevitably headed back to our family's southwest Georgia roots, a little peanut-farming town called Colquitt. *"Pull for Colquitt or Pull Out,"* read the masthead on the ironically named *Miller County Liberal*, the weekly newspaper there. After the war, Daddy pulled out with Mother in tow in order to make a better living. It must have felt a little like busting loose from prison.

Both sets of grandparents remained in Colquitt, or on family farms mighty near it, so holidays meant that long road trip. We divided the visit between maternal and paternal grandparents. And that always caused what I've come to consider classic Christmas controversies, the stuff of feuds and tantrums and migraine miseries. I believe there's no big difference between the Christmas fights of poor white Georgia crackers like us and those of Connecticut bluebloods, except in the way our disappointments and divisions were articulated. Perhaps in Connecticut Grandmother gets sullen over a cup of spice tea and engages in a virtuoso pout. The Southern way is louder. There were a lot of broken dishes involved in our spats.

What it always came down to was time. There simply wasn't enough of it. Almost nobody was ever satisfied with how we divided our limited time between the two farms, the two families. Someone always sensed a slight. Most often that someone, to be honest, was my father's mother, Lucille. And maybe she had a point. I know we children did slight her in affection. Fairly or unfairly, we feared her a little. She suffered by comparison with my mother's mother, our beloved Grannie. Grannie was a small, saintly woman who looked like a grandmother sent over from Hollywood central casting and cried when we got spankings. MaMa simply wasn't as user-friendly. You wanted to hug Grannie till the flour flew from her apron like talcum from a puff. You wanted to salute MaMa and run.

AT ANY RATE, LUCILLE, our MaMa, got mad at Christmas. Almost every year. I suppose when you've been cooking and scrubbing and wrapping and fluffing feather mattresses in anticipation of your son's visit, you have a right to be jealous of his time. "Jealous" being the key word.

Now Lucille was no fool. Moody, but in no way stupid. She used food as a weapon. In my family, that was a powerful one. We all loved to eat. She was a wonderful cook. Nobody put more Apalachicola oysters in the cornbread dressing, more rum in the fruitcake. Eating at her table was a privilege, one she withheld if you didn't do to suit her. No matter what meal we arrived for during the Christmas season, we somehow had been expected for another.

"I thought you were coming last night," MaMa would say if we arrived by noon on Christmas day. "I fried enough fish to feed an army last night and made everybody that did bother to show up wait for hours. Where were you?"

If we arrived at night, ate fish, and got up the next morning heading to the next stop, to Grannie's for the next holiday meal, it was the same drill, different food.

"I haven't even cut the fruit cake yet, Aubrey," she would say to my father in a voice full of hurt and melodrama. "You know how you love my fruit cake. I just won't bother to make one next year if you don't even take the time to eat a piece."

Lucille was nothing if not a strong-willed and feisty woman. She had buried her first husband, my father's father, when my daddy was only four. My grandfather had been kicked by a mule and died a few days later. Lucille remarried only—she was quick to tell you—out of desperation to provide for her family. Even as a child I cringed when she'd say that kind of thing in front of our kindly step-grandfather, her second husband. He would shrug it off, hide behind his newspaper and give us kids a comical smile. I guess he knew the truth when he heard it.

Lucille was tough and expected you to be. She worked harder than anyone I've ever known, including most men, and kept a cleaner house under dirtier circumstances than you'd think possible. There was the dust from the dirt road outside to contend with, plus the constantly tracking farmhands and grandchildren, not to mention the pigpen right next to the kitchen. Windows were always wide open as she had no air conditioning in my early years. And yet you could eat off of her board floor. She was a force to reckon with, and everyone knew it.

At Christmas she put gumdrops on a small plastic tree and re-plenished the candy whenever we depleted it. A live poinsettia in her chimney corner bloomed right on cue for the season. My father remembers a Christmas when she went to the trouble of making boot tracks with fireplace ashes across a sparkling clean floor to prove Santa had been there.

She was fiercely religious, too, a Primitive Baptist, which meant many things but only one that impressed me. The Baptist brand MaMa bought was the one that believed you should demonstrate your humil-ity by washing one another's feet. It was in the Good Book. Never mind that everything is in the Bible if you search hard enough—you can sacrifice live animals while playing tambourines and eating peach pits and be scripturally correct—this foot-washing business had taken hold. Mary Magdalene, after all, humbled herself before Jesus by using her long hair to wash His feet.

When you are a small child, you don't even like to wash your own feet. I found this congregational foot-washing utterly disgusting and said so, but only out of MaMa's earshot. I imagined that she probably loved it. She loved washing anything, especially feet. Many summer nights when we stayed with her, MaMa took one look at our dirty paws and poured extra Clorox in the Number Two washtub on the back steps and commenced to scrubbing *our* feet. She seemed sincerely to enjoy it. I decided, in fact, that it was the foot-washing part of the faith that decided for her which Baptist branch she'd swing from.

There were certainly many choices in the South. Even today I'm totally confused as to how so many nuanced religious doctrines emerged. Who could care enough, for instance, about the concept of sprinkling versus immersion to break off from one church and start another? How do the arguments begin? Say you're having dinner on the ground, and suddenly, over the homemade potato salad, some fool brings up predestination. Wouldn't somebody else simply say, "Look, Sam, just chill out and eat. Now is not the time or place."

People do love to argue the Good Book, however, and MaMa was the master. She was utterly convinced that all of my Southern Baptist family was going to Hell or its suburbs. We females wore pants, even shorts, after all, and cut our hair in heathenish bobs and didn't wash one another's feet, at least not in public. She told each of us on a regular basis that ours was the path to Perdition, but she did spare us grandchildren the late-night wailing with which she tortured her son. We could hear the adults crank up the theological arguments after they tucked us in and said goodnight. Usually they involved my father's reluctance to embrace *any* organized religion, but sometimes degenerated into a more specific endorsement of her brand. From the downy canyons of a feather bed in the next room, where we were expected to sleep despite the yelling and crying, it was scary stuff.

It was odd that the formidable Lucille, who was generous to a fault and who could, on good days, even be fun, saved most of her pettiness and mewling for major holidays. But she did. Tinsel and tantrums were thrown all over Christmas.

If it wasn't the timing of the visit that ignited a fight, it was the gifts. While always generous with us, Lucille displayed a legendary ungraciousness as a recipient. One year, meaning well, my mother decided her mother-in-law should be the lucky recipient of a punch bowl.

Now exactly why a plain-spoken country woman managing a hardscrabble farm would need a punch bowl I do not know. Her "dining room" was, in fact, merely a corner of the large kitchen separated from the rest of the house—by necessity, to keep the rest of the house cool while the fire in the wood-burning stove cooked the meals. As good as MaMa's cooking was, the tables she set were utilitarian. The plates sometimes matched and sometimes did not, but were always impeccably clean. In those days "presentation" was not a word you heard ad nauseam. You were lucky to have food at all, by god, and the Depression was barely down the road. A punch bowl might have been the last choice on a long list of gift possibilities.

Except my mother lived, lives, in a largely imaginary world where women the world over give weekly teas and bridal showers and use their Sunday china and every pretty dish in the cabinet to great effect. She has this need to set a perfect table. What goes on top of, or inside, the gorgeous dishes is secondary. The first of her family to graduate college, my mother majored in education, becoming, briefly and before childbirth, a teacher. But her proudest scholastic achievement was winning the Home Economics Medal at graduation, which was Olympian Gold for table-setting and such. I surmise that somewhere in her higher learning she absorbed that every proper Southern woman needs a punch bowl for charity auctions and Sunday School teas. Right after the foot-washing, you could serve petit fours and mock champagne punch.

I'm not certain that I remember this particular gift exchange, or if I simply heard the story so many times afterwards, told with angry gusto by my mother, that I merely envision it. Certainly I witnessed many similar holiday brouhahas; my grandmother was not one to whom the thought counted more than the actual gift.

Mother presented the gift—truly something she would have loved to have had herself, supposedly the test of an adequate and loving gift—and MaMa shifted the snuff in her cheek before unwrapping it, taking a moment to figure out what was in the big box. When she figured out it was a punch bowl, she kicked it and the box summarily under the bed.

The Punch Bowl Incident came to encapsulate the fractious relationship between the two women my poor father loved the most. On one hand, he had the practical, proven mother who had done what she had to do, including entering into a loveless second marriage, to raise and feed him. Then he had a raven-haired, blue-eyed wife who believed life should be officiated by Emily Post.

That vignette, the unwrapping and the kicking and the crying that resulted, might also have come to symbolize Christmas in my curly head if we hadn't, rather hastily, piled into the family sedan and pointed it toward what my mother always called "the other side of the house." We quickly pushed on the ten or so miles through the rural and lush countryside to Grannie and Pop's, where every day was Christmas for grandchildren.

The house of Clifford and Lois Houston, Grannie and Pop, is what I've tried to recreate at Christmas the rest of my life. I've never succeeded, but I've tried. No matter how many home and garden magazines I buy to peruse and use as a cheat sheet during the season, when I think of Christmas, my first thought is of their house. It wasn't fancy. Far from it. The cypress boards had once been painted white, but Pop figured painting a cypress house was like bug spray on an armadillo. The boards quickly went back to gray, Victorian curlicues and all. An iron pipe was a makeshift banister for the red brick steps Pop made himself. In summers a sycamore shaded the front yard and hydrangeas bloomed.

Somehow at Christmas, it was more beautiful. The nandina berries were blood red. The fallow fields were dark as a night sea beyond gray board fences. For the inside, Pop cut a single cedar branch from the woods, let it lap water from a saucer and strung it with lights. He tied it to a corner whatnot to keep it straight. Grannie laid the feast whatever hour we might arrive, never complaining about anything, much less the holiday schedule. If we had arrived at 2 A.M. and were hungry, she would have spread the cloth. We cousins had drawn names from a big pot back at Thanksgiving, and that decided whose Christmas present you would buy—when we were older, my favorite cousin Donna and I always managed to cheat and get one another's names.

In south Georgia sometimes Christmas could be spent outside. Balmy weather was not unusual, even in December. But when it was cold, and it could be, my grandfather fed the potbelly stove in the kitchen to stave off dampness. It was heat with a visible source, not like the central heat of today. You could see this fire, back up to it, lift your skirt and soak it in. It was heat you could trust.

The Ted Christmas is so vague and primitive a memory that it remains a gauzy mystery. I don't remember other presents that year, or whether my beloved Donna was at my grandmother's, too. I don't remember if we stayed one day or two. I mostly remember the feel of my new bedfellow, the way he'd curve into my stomach and never complain if I accidentally pushed him off the bed during the night. I carried Ted with me more years than Dr. Spock would have endorsed, literally wearing the soft fuzz off his cloth body. Grannie more than once pushed his cotton innards back inside his gut and sewed him up again.

I still have the bear, but he doesn't smell or look the same. He has that look a beloved pet gets when you start to wondering if euthanasia would be the kindest thing. For a while, I kept Ted in a cedar chest, but then took him back out to let him breathe. Once you've believed with all your heart that a thing is alive, it's hard to accept that he's not, even when you know better.

The important thing about that first Christmas memory is the total absence of malice, my obliviousness to all the adult battles and aches that surely surrounded me. Why would that year have been any different? That one Christmas was as uncomplicated and pure an experience as I'd ever have. Nobody got drunk or mad or sick. Nobody died.

And I believed with all my heart. In Santa Claus. In Jesus. In the ability of the adults to keep it between the ditches. I believed relatives all loved one another, or at least tolerated their own families for the duration of the holidays. I believed all people had plenty to eat, slept warm, that my Aunt Beulah Helen invented chocolate-covered cherries. I believed deer could fly and Ted could talk.

# 3

# The Year the World Lusted for Barbie

onnie Duncan's mother was a dish. She had the Ava Gardner look going on, with wavy black hair and a cute, voluptuous figure and the absolute confidence of a pretty woman. All of us wanted to be Cora Duncan's daughter.

Connie was my best friend, transparently convenient, since I got to stay overnight frequently at the Duncans' and have Cora tell me nice things about myself. Cora was amazingly sweet in that way. She knew I needed confidence. She would compliment my hair and eyes and posture, anything to boost my low esteem. It worked, but only as long as I was in Cora's presence. Between visits, I would forget I was worth killing.

We could stay up late at Connie's house, and try on Cora's high heels and makeup. We could generally do anything we wanted. I might never have seen Johnny Carson if it hadn't been for the Duncans, who let us park our shorty pajamas in front of the television for popcorn and inappropriate late-night adult entertainment. In the summertime Cora hosted sprinkler parties, which were in vogue before everyone and his brother had a swimming pool in the backyard. We'd run through the rainbows of cheap water in our modest swimsuits encircled with little skirts, stopping only when the watermelon was cut and served by

Cora. Sometimes we had "dress up" parties and wore glittering earbobs and evening gowns and pranced about the backyard like miniature streetwalkers.

The Duncans had an indoor dog, a poodle named Dandy, the first indoor dog I'd ever seen, and Connie's room was the stylish aqua blue and lime green of the period. Everything about their place screamed hip and happening, as opposed to my own home with its traditional furniture, something called Early American, and strict curfews and rather rigid thinking.

I think it was from the more worldly Connie that I first learned about Barbie, though in retrospect it seems as if a general alert went out in Montgomery, Alabama, and every girl between eight and eighteen suddenly had to have the doll. All at once. Barbie was on everyone's Christmas wish list in 1964. This was before there was any debate whatsoever about whether Barbie set a bad example for young ladies, what with her impossibly top-heavy figure and wardrobe from hell and total lack of math aptitude. I was eleven, almost the age when you give up dolls for jewelry and sweater sets. But I had seen Barbie. I wanted Barbie. Barbie was not so much a doll as a goal.

In Barbie's halcyon first years you bought the doll, which was wearing a strapless bathing suit, then bought the rest of her wardrobe separately. We had memorized the names of all the fancy outfits. There was "Prom Night" and "Wedding Day" and "Country Picnic." The sexiest of all was "Evening on the Town," with its black-sequined and strapless evening gown, a torch singer's duds. For some reason I wanted "Enchanted Evening" more than any of the others. It seemed more glamorously versatile.

Today you get a new doll with every outfit. Not so then. One doll, numerous outfits. Made a lot more sense.

Grannie handmade all of my Barbie doll dresses from scraps left over from the clothes she made for me. Until I was sixteen I didn't own or need a bought-ready-made dress. It didn't take much of a scrap to cover lithe Barbie, and Grannie churned out the doll clothes with regularity and great finesse.

Looking back, I should have been thrilled with the original creations, and I was grateful. I wrote my grandmother thank-you notes on flowered-y paper. But I was secretly disappointed. The homemade outfits lacked a certain sex appeal that was part and parcel of the bought-ready-made Barbie clothes. Those had a certain vampy, tight-bodice, hip-hugging, sequined allure that Grannie's neatly stitched organdy and cotton doll dresses lacked. My Barbie looked as if she had just returned from a Girl's Auxiliary meeting at the Baptist Church where the Lottie Moon Christmas offering had been discussed. The store-bought-dressed Barbie looked as if she'd had an enchanted evening all right, possibly at Ken's frat house where the boys were brewing Purple Passion punch.

Speaking of Ken, nobody I knew ever had or even wanted a Ken doll. Not even Connie. I cannot believe Mattel made the mistake of even creating a Ken doll. It was much better to imagine Barbie's mate than to see him. We were, after all, inside our Barbies, at least inside their blonde heads. Never mind I was a skinny, knock-kneed brunette with no chest and legs that were beginning to sprout ugly pubescent hair. I felt more like the stacked and blonde Barbie, with perfect ponytail and big, flirty eyes. I would decide what my boyfriend looked like, not some Mattel merchandiser.

My imaginary Ken, by the way, looked just like Steve Murphy, the son of the Pure service station owner where we gassed up the big Buick once a week. Steve was the most popular boy at Dalraida Elementary, mostly because he kept his mouth shut. That reserve, or perhaps it was real shyness, passed for cool. By not saying much, Steve achieved a mysterious allure that had me and all of my female classmates salivating. It didn't hurt that Steve also was the quarterback of the PeeWee football team and had the smoothest crew cut and deepest dimples on the squad. He was a dude worthy of our inner Barbies.

CHRISTMAS MORNING ARRIVED IN the Year of Barbie. My Barbie was in a small box that smelled of hard plastic limbs. She was perfect. The long part of her blonde ponytail felt exactly like silk, and she was wearing that trademark, strapless black and white one-piece bathing suit, the only mass-produced garment my Barbie would ever wear. With that stretchy knit swimsuit she wore toeless black heels. If you had that body, wouldn't you?

That year there was no anguish whatsoever in the decision about which toy to put in the car for the drive to Georgia. Cousin Donna and I had been exchanging letters for months discussing the Barbies we would surely get for Christmas. We were just about past the age of believing in Santa Claus, but we trusted our folks wouldn't let us down. Not this year. Not about Barbie. Not about something so life-altering as getting a doll with breasts.

Donna's family was always later getting to my grandmother's house on Christmas day than we were. We had three hours to travel, they had thirty minutes. But Donna's mother, my sweet aunt Margie, was one of those fastidious women who examined every detail of her three daughters' appearance before herding them into the car. The whole group looked parboiled and gleaming when finally they stepped out of the family auto and into the freedom that was my grandparents' house. For a few moments after arrival, their outfits were starched and ironed to perfection, their ears were clean, the hair on their heads shone like blonde halos. It wouldn't last long, but Margie got her brood there in perfect order.

The wait for Donna this time was agony. Something about "playing Barbie" was a communal sport. There are only so many times you can put your Barbie back into the box for the joy of opening it once again. Finally I saw their car pull up into the grass drive, and I ran down the red brick steps to greet Donna, waving my Barbie box like a drum major's baton.

"Did you get one?" I asked, knowing the answer and knowing she would understand the question.

"Yes!" she said, and we raced off for a private corner to compare and contrast.

Even at my insensitive age, I knew immediately that something was wrong. Her Barbie obviously wasn't. It was some cheaper, imitation doll with a ragged ponytail. Donna's attempts to smooth and wash the doll's hair had turned it the green color of an old penny. It lacked the pert, upturned nose and perfectly shaped brows of my model. This counterfeit Barbie didn't even arrive in a bathing suit, but a cotton dress. You could tell. It wasn't Mattel.

Donna handled her disappointment that day in a child's brave way. She refused to acknowledge a difference. I didn't say anything, but she knew I knew. We played. That night, under the covers, Donna bawled.

Later Aunt Margie realized the terrible mistake she had made in saving a few dollars. She bought Donna the real deal, which by then had the stylish "bubble" hairdo and was brunette. Today cousin Donna still has that doll and many of her original outfits, now worth a small fortune. I don't know what became of my Barbie, much less her wardrobe. I guess Donna's initial devastation that Christmas made her cling to the doll a little harder.

I'VE COME TO KNOW that Donna got the better gift that long-ago Christmas when I presumed to pity her. Donna's faux Barbie with green hair and lumpy features and cotton clothes forced her to deal with the truth early. We weren't ever going to dress, look, or live like Barbie. Our Dream House would come with utility bills. Prom Night often would be spent at home. Ken might take the Dream Car and run off with Midge, whom Barbie had believed was her best friend. A Country Picnic always had rain and ants. An Enchanted Evening could end in an unwanted pregnancy.

I never achieved the stylish look of Barbie. For that matter, I never achieved the nonchalant confidence of Cora Duncan. Cora would remain beautiful into her seventies. I saw her once not long ago when Connie phoned to say Cora had cancer and was not expected to live long. It was sad, returning to the little suburban Montgomery house where I'd spent so many happy childhood nights playing on the floor with Barbie dolls. I can remember imitating Cora's graceful walk, even her laugh, feeling in her presence like a different person. She had that magical effect on people.

Cora had taken up painting since I'd been around, and the walls of her home were now filled with amazing color. That living, breathing, brunette Barbie had evolved into an amazing artist and gardener, as evidenced by the view through a plate glass window into her lush and dreamy backyard. Her life, however, had not been a bed of roses. She and her husband had separated, then reunited, proving once and for all that even gorgeous women grow boring to some men. There should be a Barbie outfit for that. Disenchanted Evening.

When Cora died, hope of someday being a rare beauty died inside me. Cora had so long ago fostered that hope, telling me again and again it was just a matter of time. She detailed the features about me she found attractive, even pretty, assuring me that my beauty was in its pupa stage and needed only time's metamorphosis. I had wonderful eyes, she would stress, and a pug nose that would keep me looking younger longer. I should always wear blue or red, she said, to emphasize my coloring.

Even on her deathbed in 2009, Cora made me feel good about myself. I think that was the day I realized where her true beauty lay, and it wasn't in her porcelain skin or amazing Pocahontas eyes. She saw beauty everywhere, and in everyone, through some generous spirit that she had that most of us don't possess. Cora would have been a rare beauty without the cute clothes and good skin and high heels. There was nothing plastic about her.

# 4

# Building the Cross Fence

There was a television show called "National Velvet," based on the Elizabeth Taylor movie that was based on the book that was based on the universal love most young girls feel for horses. The horse in the show was King, of course, and I wanted to be Velvet, who was actually young actress Lori Martin, and keep a horse named King in our forty by eighty-foot suburban yard.

Pop, on a rare visit to Montgomery, bought me a plastic Breyer Shetland pony at a strip mall toy store called Toyland, and thus began the most extensive collection I would ever own of any kind until, as a middle-aged woman, I took a fancy to snow domes. Fortunately I forgot that snow domes contain water and stored them in the shed one particularly cold January, and a bunch of the domes froze and burst before that collection could get out of hand. Nothing, though, could stop the horses.

Each year with Christmas and birthday money I bought a new addition to my Breyer stable until horses covered a corner whatnot, the top of the family bookcase, and my desk. I had plastic models of pintos, Appaloosas, palominos, snow-white stallions. I owned horses galloping, rearing, nursing, and bowing. I dusted them, moved them, played with them, and cherished them. And it wasn't just the plastic horse collection that filled my every waking hour.

I would sit in live oaks trees in south Georgia with my double second cousin Marilyn Jo and trace pictures of horses from coloring books, the better to tack them to my bedroom wall. I walked almost daily several miles to a gravel pit where some fool boarded horses in a city stable without much pasture. I hero-worshiped my cousin Marshall who owned real horses and left school to become a rodeo star. Marshall once passed through Montgomery with his horse in a trailer and let me sit on top of the horse in the front yard for about five minutes.

My other riding experience came by flagging down an old black man named Jay who often rode a tall, prancing horse past Pop and Grannie's house in the summertime. If he saw us waving, Jay would stop, lift us to the saddle in front of him and trot down the road a quarter mile and back. I remember those rare rides as both smooth and terrifying, a lot like space travel.

There had been one horseback ride in Pensacola when I was tiny. One fall night a beam of light crisscrossed the sky like a silent metronome, and Daddy announced the fair was in town. Later that week he left the meat market early, and we all loaded up in the car and headed toward the source of that alien light.

I loved the fair, the cacophony of screams, barkers, and delighted squeals, the mishmash of foods and sawdust and expensive fun. I begged to ride the live ponies, sad animals with bangs in their eyes that walked around and around a ring with eager children futilely digging their heels into horseflesh to make them go faster. When it was my turn, Daddy dropped me on the saddle and the pony began its slow circle. For some reason I cannot explain, the actual ride frightened me.

I screamed, and Daddy made the man running the concession stop the horses and let me off.

But that was when I was a mere child. For Christmas the year I was twelve, and much wiser, I asked that everything I received conform to a horse theme. I thought this should make things simple, but I doubt that it did. To my mother's credit, Santa delivered. I got a horse jewelry box, a horse scarf, a book on the world-famous Lipizzaners, that awful Visible Horse I wanted so badly that it made my prayers, a horse charm for my charm bracelet that already had a saddle and a horseshoe, and probably other things I'm forgetting here. Suffice to say, I had gone whole hog for horses.

I started saving my money—except for that spent on the Breyer models, which, in that day and age didn't cost a fortune like they do now—for a horse. I would do odd jobs, cut grass, produce magic shows, pick up Coke bottles off the side of the road, or babysit for money. Nothing was too demeaning or boring if I could do the chore while daydreaming about how I'd look cantering across the countryside, jumping the occasional fence, and sleeping in the barn next to my big equine baby. I lost interest in everything else, including Barbie.

Luck was on my side. My father, a farm boy transplanted by necessity to town, desperately wanted some land. Other suburban households finagled lake real estate where they could teach their kids to water ski or barbecue Boston butts. Not us. Mother and Daddy spent weekends shopping for landlocked acres outside the city limits, asking only that it be cheap and not too far away. This hunt for land went on for years. Finally, when I was nearly thirteen, on the down slope of my passion for ponies, they found it. The seventy acres came with an old bungalow, an outhouse, over-grown pastures, falling-down fences, and more work than any sane man would tackle if he also had a day job. This was long before the trend of suburbanites looking for their roots on ten-acre storybook farms like in all the good housekeeping magazines.

In fact, it made no sense. Daddy was the first wave ashore, I'd say, of folks who grew up longing to get away from the back-breaking drudgery that was intrinsic to farming. He had left home at seventeen for Atlanta and the bright lights, working a variety of city jobs before being drafted and shipped to the Pacific. When he returned stateside, and married, he did work a short while in his hometown of Colquitt, but not on a farm. Instead he purposely chose a trade, as a butcher, and parlayed that into a real career with many upwardly mobile moves.

Why he suddenly decided that farming could be a hobby, especially a desirous one, remains a mystery to me. Maybe my horse fetish had something to do with it. Daddy and Mother claimed that it did. Maybe, but I doubt it. My parents were good, but not doting. I think that part was strictly coincidence. I believe by the time he'd labored for The Man for twenty years, Daddy realized the truth: There are worse things than waking to your own list of chores, and worse work than that which leaves you with sore muscles and a free mind at the end of the day. What wears us out at any job is the politics of it, whether we are cutting up meat or fine-tuning a newspaper obituary.

By the time Daddy bought the farm, my older sister JoAnne wanted nothing to do with it. She wanted to stay in town where the telephone might ring or a girlfriend might want to go shopping. I was on the fence, at the cusp of puberty. I still clung to my tomboy status, wearing Lumberjack Meat Company shirts that a bacon broker had given Daddy, pretending not to be at all interested in boys, mowing the lawn while my sisters helped with the dusting. But by the time the land deal was secured and a real horse seemed a real possibility, I was wondering at the monster I had created.

All I had to do before actually getting the horse, the one I'd saved for and dreamed of, was help my father build a cross fence, that being the fence between us and the neighbors on our north. The fence between us and the road was done.

Daddy spent his two weeks' vacation farming now instead of fishing. And each summer morning I'd get up, climb into a blue pickup held together by right-wing bumper stickers, and ride to the farm that was seventeen miles from our Montgomery home. My job was to shovel sand into the hole around the post after Daddy used posthole diggers to create said hole. It was slow, hard work, and I was secretly beginning to wonder if a horse was the be-all to end-all. There was one powerful incentive, and it wasn't a horse. Every now and then Daddy let me drive the truck. I would move the old rattletrap a few paces ahead, pushing the clutch in and staying in first gear, or, at most, second. One day I mashed the gas pedal instead of the clutch, lurching ahead, running over baby pine trees and odd posts, scared out of my wits and sure it would be my last time ever behind the wheel.

"You didn't hurt a thing," my father said through the truck window, when I finally found the brake. "You probably knocked as many dents out of this truck as you knocked in it."

He could be kind like that when you least expected it, or, at the opposite extreme, lose his formidable temper for some minor infraction. Working with Daddy kept you on your toes, and I felt a little sorry for those he supervised at his real job. They must be nervous wrecks, I decided.

For lunch we'd eat whatever Mother had put in a brown sack, and then usually for a few minutes we napped, side by side, sitting up, in the truck. We were exhausted by the labor and heat. I'm not sure how long the cross fence took to build—couldn't have been much longer than two weeks, Daddy's normal vacation time—but it seemed to take forever. True to his word, when the fence was finished, we went to pick out a horse. The head of Winn-Dixie, my father's company, was one Tine Davis, a legendary grocer and weekend rancher. He had a Quarter Horse stable nearby, and he liked my father. A deal was struck for a registered Quarter Horse—without his papers—a soda-colored gelding named CocoMo.

The day they delivered CocoMo should have been the best day of my life. God knows I'd made enough passionate noise about wanting a horse, a real horse, and somehow, through great parental effort and expense, it had happened. The money I'd saved to buy a horse went toward the saddle, a Western, two-tone beauty that cost almost as much as the animal it would straddle.

Along with CocoMo came a Shetland pony named Rebel for my younger sister Sheila. She'd never been the type to carry on about her dreams like I, and she had never said anything one way or the other about wanting a horse. In fact, I don't think Sheila said two entire sentences until she was twenty-eight. But that day, the day the horses came, she hopped on the cantankerous, aptly named Rebel and became an instant horsewoman. How I hated her.

I, on the other hand, who had spent so many years immersed in imaginary horses—the clean kind whose ears you whispered instructions to and whose manes you braided with blue grosgrain ribbon—discovered too late that the real deal scared the hell out of me. Why, it was nothing like sitting on the wide limb of a live oak with a lap full of tracing paper and a crayon sharpener. It was nothing akin to cruising Toyland for the newest Breyer horse. All of a sudden it was do or die, so I pretended to be happy instead of knee-knocking nervous, and slowly took the reins.

Sheila and I test-drove the new horseflesh around the pasture, Sheila grinning and having the time of her life, me nervously hanging onto the horn of the hard-won Western saddle. At first it went well. I clucked, CocoMo moved out, slowly and calmly. Could it be this simple? Hanging on was all there was to it. When we started back toward the barn, however, it was as if the sluggish CocoMo had had a fire lit under his blond tail. He flew back over the terrain, startling me and shaking the little confidence I'd found while familiarizing myself with his formerly slow pace. I might as well have been three again, hanging on for dear life on that pony at the Pensacola fair.

When I got off the saddle, the inside of my thighs was covered in a lather the color of beer foam, a sight I'd never noticed on Velvet when she hopped off of King on the television show that got me into this mess. This was dirty business, this horse stuff. And now I was stuck, at least through high school, with the biggest pet in the world to take care of, one you couldn't flush down the toilet if he died.

CocoMo, in his defense, was a relatively good and solid horse who responded to neck reining, meaning you didn't have to do anything but touch a rein to his neck in the direction you wanted to head. Other than the accelerated trips home to the barn—which never ended—he was a good smooth ride.

Rebel, on the other hand, lost no opportunity to buck or rub Sheila off on the barbed-wire fence, or head toward a low limb to try and knock her off. It never fazed her. But because I was older and, in theory, more experienced, Daddy would order Sheila off the horse and put me in the saddle.

"Show him who's boss," Daddy would coach, meaning that I should be the one in charge. Ha. Whatever Rebel wanted to do, he did. Once we ended up in the center of Daddy's fish pond, me sitting there stupidly staring, up to my bony knees in tepid water, Rebel turning his head back toward me with a toothy and churlish smile.

Rebel's rebellion proved a way out for me eventually. Confounded by the pony, who wouldn't respond to my father's yelling or occasional lashing with a belt, Daddy took decisive action. Rebel was sold to another poor soul who didn't know that Shetland ponies are the absolute worst kind of ride for a younger child. Size isn't everything. That left only CocoMo, and I gladly let Sheila take over the horse the same way she'd inherited my Barbie doll and my bicycle. What a relief it was to relinquish the duties of riding, grooming, feeding, and otherwise worrying over the big horse. I could go back to dreaming, which is what I do best, and deciding what my new line of hobby might be.

# 5

# Armed and Dangerous

I t wasn't as if I had never gotten guns for Christmas before. There was, notably, the year of the cowgirl outfit, when Santa Claus, in an extraordinarily generous mood, brought me two metal cap guns, holsters, a cowgirl skirt and shirt with arrow pockets, a felt hat, and fancy boots with tin-foil adornments.

I ran into my bedroom, put on the loot and came out blazing. I was cute as the dickens.

Now, in my teens, already perceived by my junior high school classmates as a real nerd because I played the accordion and wore my hair cut like Buster Brown, I decided to reprise my gun-toting career. For the life of me, I cannot remember why I decided I wanted a pellet gun for Christmas. I just did. Because they were there. Because it might impress my father. Because if you couldn't be a popular cheerleader, you might as well be a tomboy.

The oddest thing: I was a good shot. An amazingly good shot. I'm not proud of this now, but I was then. That Christmas during the obligatory grandparents' visit, my Pop said he'd give me fifty cents if I could hit a red-headed woodpecker pecking away on a dead tree in the back pasture. I spent the money on candy in town that afternoon. And besides the tin cans I practiced on, I could pop turtles in my father's fish pond with deadly accuracy. And I helped keep down the swallow population in the rafters of the barn one pellet at a time.

I was an impressionable kid. I probably was influenced by my new best friend Patricia Yancey, who probably never even owned a Barbie doll. She was the real deal, not just some soft-bellied girl pretending to be tough. She was fearless. Patricia spent Saturdays with her father on their farm, riding horses bareback, picnicking on the railroad trestle, and, when in town, using the city's storm sewers as her personal water park. Probably it was Patricia who thought my getting a pellet gun for Christmas would be a good idea so she could borrow it. So I did.

There's a photograph of me Christmas morning. Unfortunately. I am wearing a pleated gold wool skirt, green knee socks, awful gray Hush Puppies that my mother preferred to all other shoes, a little brown British driver's cap that was vaguely in style at the time, and I am holding my new gun. Of all the awful pictures of me taken during my lifetime—and there are many, including, especially, newspaper mug shots—that one is the worst. I look like a cross-dressing, gun-toting British chap who can't decide on a color scheme for his wardrobe. In fact, he is colorblind.

The gun was one of those things you could slide under the bed when friends came, and usually I did, unless the friend was Patricia. We both wore our Lumberjack T-shirt uniforms and lined up pea cans along the back fence and pretended we were legendary sharpshooters. We also killed the occasional cardinal.

Patricia and I often spent hours in the new Montgomery discount store called Gaylord's. It was a precursor to Wal-Mart and within walking distance of our homes. We thought it was absolutely wonderful.

We tried on every swimsuit on the rack, and bought popcorn to eat while we walked every aisle and rummaged every counter. We never bought anything but the popcorn. One day we finally had exhausted the possibilities and were leaving, our big white plastic purses on our respective arms. The manager, an officious little twit I can see right now, stopped us before we could get outside.

"Open your purses," he demanded. Which we did. Inside mine was a dirty hairbrush, a coin purse, and a Bible tract from the Baptist church. Patricia's bag looked much the same, I'm sure.

The manager didn't say, "I'm sorry, just checking," or "Kiss my foot."

We were mortified. I, of course, was horrified that anyone would possibly suspect me, the good little Baptist with perfect attendance in Training Union, of shoplifting. I couldn't wait to tell my father, whose legendary temper would fix that fellow for sure. What I didn't expect was to be involved in the resolution.

When we told Daddy what happened, he loaded Patricia and me in his car, drove straight to Gaylord's, and found the manager. "Apologize to them," my father said in a voice that implied the manager could look for his teeth in the parking lot if he failed to deliver.

As satisfying as the outcome was, it just about ruined shopping for me forever. Even today when I'm in a store without a buggy, I hold the item I want to purchase out of front of me as if I'm a Wise Man carrying frankincense to the Baby Jesus.

But all the misadventures involving Patricia were true bonding experiences. When the next school year came, I expected our exclusive club of two to continue, with weekends spent jumping off the railroad trestle, and weekdays doing weird things like taking turns cleaning a marshmallow cream jar with our fingers or trying to start chemical fires with our chemistry sets. What I didn't expect was to see Patricia in the junior high girls' restroom applying white lipstick and mascara.

"You wear mascara?" I asked in horror.

"Only every once in a while," she said through her cadaver lips. "Want to try some?"

I most certainly did, but I suddenly became, in the face of her solitary experimentation, the super prude. I sensed something was happening that excluded me, and it hurt. And I didn't know the half of it. Not yet. Patricia and I had both signed up to try out for cheerleading, but we were such long shot candidates that the popular girls even grew charitable and tried to help us improve our stances. Your stance was mighty important, right up there with your split and your jump.

What the popular girls hadn't counted on was the fact that the judges for the cheerleader competition came from outside the school. The objective outsiders had no idea who wore what to last year's prom, or who was considered the shoo-in for the squad and who had no chance whatsoever, not in this lifetime.

I should have been so happy when Patricia won. She was, after all, another one like me, a geek with a wide tomboyish streak, not really one of the cool, beautiful people who spent the break between class periods in the restroom applying chalky white lipstick.

I was not happy. Not one little bit. The earth shifted, and I was left on the dark side of the abyss while Patricia floated off into a whole other stratum. Her year on the cheerleading squad virtually ended our friendship, and it was my fault. She wanted to remain friends. She might even have paved the way for me to lunch with the Bass Weejuns crowd, if only I had let her. I was far too stubborn for that.

I struggled along with girls from the Latin Club and the other

Untouchables, living for the day when we'd leave that purgatory called junior high and go to high school. I'd been told that there assets like brains and subtle beauty were much in demand, that bra size and store-bought clothes took a back seat to scholarship. If ever I remember who told me that, she's dead meat.

# 6

# Born Again

I got religion again with a vengeance when Brad McClain dumped his girlfriend Belinda for Jesus. Brad was the best-looking boy at Robert E. Lee High School, bar none. He had fathomless brown eyes and black hair that touched his collar. He wasn't big, not jock big, just the perfect size when you walked beside him. He looked a lot like the actor Robbie Benson, who had long lashes and such soulful eyes he seemed always to be crying.

Brad and I were friends. Good friends. Maybe even best friends for a while. Which is not a good thing, not if you want a boy to think of you romantically. I once had tutored him in algebra, which was a joke since I had no math skills whatsoever. I would have tutored Brad McClain in ancient Hebrew or Sanskrit if he'd asked, which, come to think of it, would have made more sense for me to be explaining than algebra. Brad and I also worked together on the staff of *The Stars and Bars*, the school newspaper, using the term "work" loosely since all we did was leave campus early in the name of selling advertising.

The revival happened overnight, or so it seemed. Normally Brad's dramatic conversion wouldn't have mattered much to anyone but beautiful Belinda, who took being jilted for Jesus pretty hard. But Brad had this way of multiplying his women like loaves and fishes, and religion was the killer addition to his romantic sheen. His crusade for converts transformed the immediate landscape, especially when Brad began a series of youth revivals that lit up east Alabama's back roads like a meteor. A gang of us, high school females mostly, followed him to rural pulpits in two-bit churches that had never seen crowds like Brad could draw.

The adults were genuinely alarmed. It was one thing to go to church—that was requisite—but quite another to take it all so seriously. Church was a club to most adults back then. You paid your dues and made business and social contacts. Members in good standing went to Heaven. There was certainly nothing political about it the way it's become today.

But Brad's crusade was Peter, Paul, and the Pied Piper all tied up together. This was something so sexy and passionate and flat-out that adults couldn't help but be distressed. Teenagers with long hair were praying over their pepperoni pizza and speaking in tongues instead of slang. The graffiti in the school restrooms suddenly said things like "One Way!" and "Jesus Saves" instead of "Mister Carter is an SOB." It was scary stuff.

I personally endured my father's wrath when he returned from a week-long work trip and Mother ratted me out for blatantly disobeying her and going to a youth revival on a school night. I was a real wild child. It was the last time I remember my father punishing me, if you don't count that hurtful disapproval that parents never quit meting out in phone calls and averted eyes. But I didn't care. I would have parted the Red Sea to get to a Brad McClain performance.

And that's what it was. A glorious, theatrical, romantic act. Did I mention romantic? He would stand in the front of those little sanctuaries cajoling and really crying till every female in the joint had

come forward sobbing to accept Jesus or rededicate herself to the
Lord's work. Either one meant Brad would take your shaking hands
in his and hold them. He would then kneel with you and touch his
black head to yours in an intimate moment that nobody else could
share. "Praise Jesus!" he would shout, ending the brief intimacy with
a euphoric shout that rocked the building. Next?

Brad took to wearing his revival white suits, white shoes, and
tangerine-colored shirts to school. That is, he wore them when he
bothered to attend school. He missed so many days off evangelizing his
senior year that his parents had to do some fancy talking to convince
administrators that he qualified for graduation. The Lord won.

Graduate he did, clutching his diploma with one hand and waving
the other in the One Way salute. By then all of Brad's disciples, including me, were wearing gigantic crosses around our necks instead of our
boyfriends' class rings. The bigger the cross, the better. The Christian
cross was as stylish as the peace symbol that had become the best-
selling by-product of the Vietnam War. I remember wearing mine the
night I let my boyfriend slide into First Base in the backseat of a VW
bug. Did I mention that Brad's brand of religion was somewhat less
judgmental than the kind I'd grown up with, a lot looser about things
like sex and music? My regular Baptist church had recoiled in horror
the year a young minister of music added drums to the Christmas
cantata, since drums were a rock and roll staple, and rock and roll
was the Devil's domain. Brad preached against premarital sex, but I
don't think he really expected us to pay much attention to that part
of his sermon. His lips said "No, no!" but his Maxwell House eyes
said "Yes, yes!"

At Lee High we normally stood in a restroom's fog of cigarette
smoke and Aqua Net, making the most of the few minutes between

classes to swap juicy tidbits of gossip. We knew which cheerleaders were pregnant. A pregnancy's hard to hide while turning cartwheels. Talk was always about the girls who would, the girls who would not, and the boys who asked.

Suddenly we were the sanctimonious set, holier than thou or anyone else. Gossip faltered. There was nothing to tell. We followed Brad's lead and broke up with anyone we felt the least bit of sexual attraction for, lest we be tempted. Didn't much matter. All of us were in love with Brad, anyhow, and no weak substitutes would do. Even the males in our group were smitten. Several of them became youth ministers, following Brad's example. I would sometimes go out with a preacher boy named Charles, but he was Deuteronomy to Brad's Revelation.

We put the Christ back in Christmas that year in a big way, what with our ostentatious prayers at the Pizza Hut, our One Way greetings in the hall, and intercom devotionals that lasted past the prescribed five minutes. We were downright obnoxious in our piety. Worst thing was, I knew better.

Even as a young child I had always dreaded feeding The Hungry at Christmas. Or at least our Southern Baptist, Sunday School approach to feeding the hungry. I believe the hungry hated it, too.

An entire Sunday School class would pile into the teacher's boat of a car. Slowly we would make our way through some neighborhood we did not know, that for certain was not ours. Our intrepid leader would verify the address from a slip of paper that the church office had assigned her, park the Buick by the curb, if indeed the neighborhood had curbs and gutters, then wrestle a big cardboard box out of the trunk. In the box were canned goods—often things that our own families didn't like to eat, like beets or rutabagas—maybe a ham, some fruit, a bag of hard peppermints. Whatever we'd collected during the past couple of weeks.

Then all of us, the entire class, marched to the door. The hungry were always expecting us. I remember the quiet exchanges, the mumbled thanks, the command appearance of big-eyed children from some back room. All of us kids—little Baptist visitors in wool pleats and studied smiles, the embarrassed children of need—all of us would shuffle and stare at our feet while the adults exchanged a few words. One year a mother made her children perform a carol; they had rehearsed. Reedy voices sang of dashing through the snow, laughing all the way. What snow? In Alabama? What laughter? What the hell?

Even as a child, I knew the poor shouldn't have to sing for their supper.

Christmas had become more about what you got from your boy-friend than Santa Claus. My main squeeze, the one I hadn't cut off even for Brad and Jesus, was a neighbor boy who was out of high school and working at a service station while awaiting his assignment from the Naval Reserves. That year he took his hard-earned cash and bought me purple corduroy bell-bottoms and a lavender turtleneck. The jeans laced up with shoestrings in the front and the back. The clothes looked like something Cher would wear. They were stylish and tight-fitting and different from the Mother-sanctioned clothes I normally wore, which often were hand-me-downs from my older sister JoAnne, who had conservative taste and would invest her allowance in one nice beige linen dress while I opted for five cheap T-shirts.

I loved the outfit my boyfriend bought and wore it for our Christmas Eve date.

I remember wondering what Brad would think about it.

7

# Cold Chapel, Cold Feet

We fell in love while slow-dancing to Joe Cocker at a student newspaper Christmas party in an Auburn catfish restaurant. Jimmy Johnson's longtime sweetheart and fiancée had to be somewhere else that night, leaving the door wide open for me. Moral of this story: Never miss a Christmas party.

I had known him professionally, you might say, for three years, watched him in the wee hours bent over his drawing paper, rendering cartoon fillers for whatever blank space we found ourselves with at 2 A.M. on deadline. He was a genius. I knew it the first time I saw him in action and have not changed my mind in the thirty-eight years since.

He would sit, pen behind one ear, quietly studying the newsprint hole that needed filling, silently deciding the best line art for the situation. The *Auburn Plainsman* staff never stumped him. From desperation would come lively cartoons in the tradition of Thurber and Schulz. He could write well, too.

Party night he looked different somehow, and, before the long evening was over, his dark eyes drew me shamelessly into embrace. I remember what he wore. I remember what I wore, though I had borrowed the outfit from a college suitemate and never had it on again. Which maybe means I remembered to return it.

Suddenly it was as if all of the honest admiration I'd had for Jimmy in the newspaper office melted down like Mother's boxed paraffin and was poured into a heart-shaped mold. It all happened quickly, spontaneously. It was mutual. Given the location, it was a little greasy.

It was also inconvenient, considering the wedding invitations for Jimmy and his high school sweetheart already had been printed, though, mercifully, not yet mailed. He came that close to a clean getaway. It was tough for him, telling her, and, of course, a true heartbreak for the poor girl. I felt some remorse, but not enough to change my course. I loved him.

We waited a year to marry, only because my father vehemently objected when Jimmy went to him and explained we intended to make it official the summer before my senior year. Daddy lost it. I was to graduate before I married, he insisted. Out of respect, and fear, we agreed to wait. But we didn't say for how long. We secretly planned our wedding for the next December 6, the anniversary date of that fateful party that changed our lives.

The wedding was early in the morning at Georgia's groomed and golden Callaway Gardens, known for its golf course and man-made beach. In 1974 you could rent the Callaway chapel with its walls of stained glass for two hundred dollars. That price included a minister to officiate and an organist.

I had been been mightily influenced by the Franco Zeffirelli film, *Romeo and Juliet*, and wanted to wear red velvet and keep the Shakespearean romance in the ceremony. I abhorred the wedding style of the day, the Baptist kind, which always included a dozen bridesmaids, shoes that matched your dress, and a boring and dry reception following. I didn't even want a photographer lining up people and spoiling the mood. I wanted the minister to officiate, the minimum two friends as witnesses, and us. Brides never get what they want.

Jimmy's parents asked to come and they were too sweet for us to refuse them. Which meant my parents had to be invited as well, though they remained lukewarm at best about the idea of marriage before my graduation. Jimmy had graduated the year before, but I still had two more scholastic quarters to finish, plus the *Plainsman* to edit. I had been elected editor the spring before.

The red dress, of course, wouldn't do with parents in attendance. Red indicated sin, which, of course, meant sex.

There were glitches. There always are. Jimmy, ever the procrastinator, forgot about the need for a marriage license until the day before the wedding. The Hamilton County courthouse was closed, but somebody told us how to get to the home of the probate judge. The judge reluctantly agreed to meet Jimmy the next morning, our wedding day, and take care of it. We hoped he would remember the chore on a Saturday. Unsure that he would and that we would actually get the license, we asked a fellow *Plainsman* staffer, a rather dignified-looking fellow named Frank, if he would pretend to be a minister if the need arose. Frank dutifully rehearsed.

Fortunately, used to acting on deadline, Jimmy drove to the courthouse and got the license. Frank, the faux minister, was off the hook.

There also was the matter of my cold feet. I desperately wanted to marry Jimmy, but something about admitting the marriage in public and print gave me pause. I had, after all, been an outspoken critic of women who go to college only to find a husband. I'd railed against what we then called the MRS degree. Now here I was, the infamous

(by Auburn standards) women's libber, getting married *before* I graduated. So, a few days before the wedding, I balked.

"I don't have a long slip," was how I, ever the coward, explained it
to Jimmy. I had bought a beautiful long dress off the rack for $25 to
wear for the ceremony. It was ivory with macramé lace, the perfect
look for a wedding in the woods, I thought. It was the next best thing
to a red Juliet dress.

Jimmy, being Jimmy, went to the local department store, braved
the lingerie section and bought me a long slip. It was the sweetest
thing a boy, a man, had ever done for me. I had no more excuses and
felt my feet grow warm.

It was December cold that morning, and the holly bushes were
wearing their Christmas berries. Beautiful, but frigid. Callaway Gardens
maintenance had forgotten to turn on the heat in the stone wedding
chapel in the woods. It didn't much matter to the two of us. The organist
played the songs I had chosen—"Morning Has Broken," "Oh, What
a Beautiful Morning," and "Sunshine on My Shoulders"—and the
majestic music filled the fairy-tale woods of the beautiful and empty
grounds of Callaway. About fifteen guests, most of them uninvited,
shuddered as Jimmy and I stood at the rock altar and exchanged vows.
The wildflower bouquet I had chosen did not arrive in time for the
ceremony. The minister we'd rented used the "obey" part of the vows
and everyone in attendance wondered if I'd stomp out. My *Plainsman* columns had given me a rather misleading reputation as a fierce
feminist. Jimmy knew better.

The preacher did remember to add the verses from Ecclesiastes
that I'd asked for: *Two are better than one . . . if two lie together, then
they have heat: but how can one be warm alone?*

My Baptist upbringing wasn't totally wasted. For in that cold chapel, we needed to feel some kind of heat. Immediately after the ceremony, the two of us fled to the parking lot and Jimmy's green Pinto. Because of some typically malfunctioning Pinto part, it was necessary each time you cranked the car to raise the hood of the car and push a button. Jimmy had carefully done all this before the wedding in case guests followed us to the "getaway" car. Nobody did.

We had chosen our honeymoon destination by looking at a map of the southeastern United States. We knew we wanted a seacoast town, but Florida was tacky and North Carolina too far. We had to be able to drive to our destination in one day. We only had a long weekend off before Jimmy went back to his reporting job at the *Opelika-Auburn News*, and I went back to school and my responsibilities at the *Plainsman*. Neither of us had ever been to the Georgia coast, but the names Sea Island and St. Simons Island sounded lovely, mystical, romantic. We made up our minds to drive there. After all, we had nearly one hundred dollars to spend.

First, though, we stopped at a Hardee's in Fort Valley, Georgia, to get out of our wedding duds and into something more comfortable. We ordered French fries for lunch and kept trucking, now wearing blue jeans and big smiles. The tension of my disapproving parents and the goofy for-rent minister and a photographer who showed up unsolicited, all of that was in the rearview mirror. It was just the two of us, bound for the ocean. The sea was one of a million things we agreed on. The mountains, we would say time and again, are beautiful, but they just sit there. The ocean is constantly in motion.

We stayed two nights at a motel called the Queen's Court, the only affordable place on St. Simons. We had no idea of the reputation of neighboring Sea Island, really just a bayou away, as the playground of millionaires and home of the famous Cloister Hotel. We liked St.

Simons the best anyhow, and couldn't believe our luck, romping for a weekend on a picturesque island that seemed downright idyllic. It still had a few dirt roads, and lots of empty space, and a long pier that was a community gathering place. Normal people seemed to inhabit it, along with rich Yankees. You could see working shrimp boats in the distance. Best of all there was a lighthouse, a gorgeous specimen with a red-brick keeper's cottage.

Looking around, we noticed there was one thing missing. There was no newspaper. Not a real one, anyhow. Oh, there were a couple of advertising shoppers, which we dismissed out-of-hand. We still had journalism school stars in our eyes. And there was a strong, established newspaper on the mainland, the *Brunswick News*. But it struck us that St. Simons was its own community, a dozen miles and a world away from the more workaday atmosphere of Brunswick. And any community, we figured, could use its own newspaper.

We fell in love with the island on our honeymoon. We fell in love with the idea of starting our own weekly newspaper. After all, P. C. Burnett, one of our Auburn professors, had told us again and again: "All you need to start a newspaper is a typewriter."

We believed him.

Somehow, in the glow of young and new love, on an island named for a saint, it seemed quite possible. Instead of shopping, eating out, or staying in bed all day, we spent our brief time on the island taking notes, checking out the journalistic possibilities. I would graduate in June, Jimmy would give notice, and we'd be back on the Golden Isles of Georgia before the next Christmas. As long as we were taking vows, we vowed as much.

The main thing Jimmy and I had in common was the ability to think outside of a box. Where that came from I'll never know. Both of us had grown up in ultraconservative Alabama, the children of typical Southern parents, Baptists all. But we were dreamers. We dreamed big. Many nights in the *Plainsman* office we'd be the last two staffers standing, or not standing as the case actually was. We took catnaps on stacks of last week's issue, comparing goals. Jimmy wanted desperately to become a cartoonist. I wanted to be a syndicated columnist.

But owning a prosperous weekly in paradise would do nicely, too, come to think of it.

"My, you're brave," more than one friend said when we told them what we planned. We had no idea what they were talking about. Brave? What was brave about plying your trade in paradise? What, for god's sake, was the big deal?

# 8

# Christmas Sunset

I have a strong right arm. Even now, with that disgustingly flabby middle-aged skin that hangs down when it used to be taut, my right arm is the go-to arm for cranking or lifting or getting things done. I've simply used it a lot more over the years than I have my left arm. And at no time was it more in service than for twenty-six weeks on that dollop of paradise called St. Simons Island.

We threw three thousand newspapers out the window of that slime green Pinto on Christmas Day 1975. I let fly out the passenger window and was deadly accurate. I could hit a front porch from fifty paces. You had to be accurate when you were throwing freebies to rich people, mostly well-to-do, retired Yankee residents who had entire crews to keep their lawns tidy and certainly wouldn't want to find last week's newspaper on the roof or in the oleander bushes. We even threw papers on Sea Island, where you were supposed to get permission to sneeze.

I didn't know it on that pre-dawn Christmas run, but the ink I was throwing with my strong right arm was smeared across the last issue of the short-lived *St. Simons Sun*, a weekly newspaper Jimmy and I had started from scratch the June before with another recent Auburn journalism graduate, David Nordness. We honored our honeymoon vows.

We might not have finished the task that bleak December morning if we had known there was no tomorrow for *The Sun*. We did know one thing for certain. We were completely out of money. The seed money our Alabama editor friend Millard Grimes had given us—an amazing, or so it seemed at the time, $10,000—had evaporated faster than dew on palmetto. Most of it had gone to pay the printing costs in Jesup, Georgia, where a young but entirely unsympathetic editor named Dink NeSmith was, as the old joke goes, "printing money" on his father's press. Dink charged penalties for every moment we were late—we were always late—managing to exhaust our budget and enthusiasm at the same time. None of the original Millard money went for salaries; we didn't pay ourselves anything except the rent money the entire seven months we were there.

Dave Nordness, a bright and capable fellow whose main job it was to sell advertising for *The Sun*, got burned out on journalism forever and left the island paradise in October to return to school for an engineering degree. We didn't blame him. When we had toasted to our success back in Auburn, nobody had anticipated an unpaid year of drudgery. We knew, after all, how to write, report, take photographs, figure ad percentages, write headlines, and typeset. We knew it all.

For food that year we depended on "swap-outs," a newspaper advertising term that meant trading advertising space for goods and services. Of course that meant some business had to want your space and you, in turn, had to need their service to make the arrangement palatable. Our main "swap-out" was with a dark and cozy little seafood restaurant and bar in St. Simons's fabled and quaint downtown Village. The eatery was called The Inward Point. The menu was delectable but limited, and for at least four years after *The Sun* failed, I had trouble looking at a shrimp, much less eating one. Ditto blue cheese dressing, the house specialty. I look back at photos from that period and am amazed how skinny I became in the course of seven months. You could see my ribs beneath the bodices of my favorite rayon dresses. I looked like a relatively well-dressed Biafran refugee. And I remember feeling hungry and sleepy the entire time we lived on St. Simons. Whenever I sat still for more than a few minutes, I fell asleep. Often when driving the newspapers from Jesup back to the island, we'd take turns, one driving while the other two partners slept. One day, after everyone had failed to stay awake at the wheel, we simply pulled to the side of the road and all took a nap at once. What a strange sight that must have been. Three disheveled comrades, sleeping in a compact car crammed with thousands of newspapers.

I think we went to the beach three times in all those weeks, and all three times late at night once our work was done. One of those beach nights, meant as a romantic respite for newlyweds married a little over a year, ended with me falling asleep in the sand. I was too exhausted to mind the sand, much less feel romantic. The only year I lived on a resort island was the only year I had no suntan.

It was a life-altering experience, starting a weekly newspaper. There were lessons learned during those twenty-six weeks, most of them obvious. My personal favorite is this: some people pay their bills while others do not. Amazingly, bars were among the most dependably conscientious ad customers. Bars always paid up. And on time. The bartender might find the cash for the ad in his own boot, but you got your money. Fancy gift shops, on the other hand, were slow to ante up for advertising. Our ad account with the fanciest commercial establishment on St. Simons, a high-end furniture store, still owes us money. I have, over the years, resisted the urge to return to the island and load up a fine leather sofa and matching loveseat.

We also learned that it's difficult to be your own boss. We'd been taught enough at journalism school to produce a good-looking, readable editorial product, but the business end of the newspaper business, that we'd dismissed as a necessary evil, was a complete mystery to all of us. I discovered, much to my dismay, that I am incapable of selling anything, including ice cubes on the beach. I would approach the manager of some swell island store, stammer, look at my feet and forget the spiel I'd rehearsed. "You wouldn't want to buy an ad in a brand new unproven publication called the *St. Simons Sun*, would you?" Of course not. Who would after that introduction? Then I'd buy a little something to thank the merchant for not giving me the boot, leaving the store richer and us in the hole.

Fortunately both Jimmy and Nordness were better salesmen—Jimmy only marginally so—and, thanks to my father, I had an "in" with the Winn-Dixie grocery chain. That weekly grocery ad came camera-ready for every week *The Sun* managed to survive. And it helped us survive. For a short while.

There were some wonderful moments, though, foremost the day the first issue rolled off the rented press. It was as close as I'll ever get to giving birth. It was a birth. We had finagled a front-page interview with then-Governor George Busbee, jumped headfirst into coverage of a monumental lawsuit involving public versus private beach access, introduced ourselves to the readership with personal columns, and rendered a predictable shot of the St. Simons lighthouse in a blue duotone.

What a moment. Holding that broadsheet in my hands was as big a thrill as a tired mother ever felt cradling a child. Or close enough to do me. And there were other stellar days: The one in July when our sign was delivered and hung. (I still have the sign.) The Fourth of July in the Village with spectacular fireworks over the ocean. The day our first bride submitted her wedding write-up, which is the surest path to establishment for a newspaper, getting brides and their mothers to come to you for coverage. The day the storied and staid Sea Island Company that owned the Cloister Hotel ordered and paid for a subscription. The night on neighboring Jekyll Island when the Georgia Press Association recognized us as a true journalistic entity.

We were, if I do say so myself and defensively, only a few years ahead of ourselves. In less than a year, a peanut farmer from south Georgia would become president and put St. Simons on the international map when he located his little White House in its peripheral marsh. We had badly underestimated a couple of journalistically dicey but thriving "shoppers," one of them run by a friendly and healthy dilettante, the other by nastily competitive women partners. None of them knew a thing about journalism—except how to survive.

*The Sun* came and went behind economic clouds, but somehow there was always something to throw out the car window come Tuesday, then Wednesday, finally Thursday, morning. Over the months we added a sports columnist, who wrote for the glory, and a marine editor, Miles Baker, old salt and retired professional photographer who also worked for the exposure and added some real class to the new newspaper's feature shots. We had a subscription contest and gave the winner a bike. After Nordness deserted, we enlisted an ad salesman from the local radio station who worked hard and effectively—and on commission. You could buy a full page in *The Sun* for $125. Another few months and we might have made a go of it, but too much happened too late in the game. Jimmy and I were exhausted.

That 1975 Christmas Day was not altogether sad. Even that last day had its sunny moments. After throwing our usual complement of three thousand papers—free because so few had been quick to subscribe to the fledgling publication, and we had to be able to tell advertisers that lots of folks would see their ad—we returned to our apartment on Ocean Boulevard to exchange gifts and eat a big breakfast. Two young people can do worse than spend Christmas morning eating real bacon a block off the Atlantic. I've never again lived on an Ocean Boulevard, or, for that matter, a boulevard.

It was a regular O. Henry Christmas. Sort of. Neither of us had any money, but we had rather ingeniously managed to find gifts for one another.

Jimmy is the best gift-giver I've ever known, bar none, male or female, sweetheart or friend. He had this instinctive knack for knowing what you wanted before you knew, plus an artist's eye for beauty. He once bought me a ten-speed bicycle and, at the same time, dramatically announced "our" plans to bike the length of North Carolina's Outer Banks. For our first-year anniversary he gave me the gold wedding band we couldn't afford when we married. Our first Christmas, the year before *The Sun*, he showered me with gifts, most memorably a wonderful watercolor of myself in my bulky blue robe typing a newspaper story at our kitchen table.

This time he had worked a swap-out with a shopping mall music store on the mainland, filling the Pinto with albums by every musician I'd ever mentioned or admired. I had, quite suddenly and much to my surprise and delight, an astonishing music library. Not bad for a couple of newlyweds with no salary between them.

I, too, had finagled a gift. I had answered a phone call one day at the humble and messy *St. Simons Sun* office, expecting a complaint, which was the only kind of phone call that ever rang. Instead, it was a young friend of ours, a brilliant boy named ChaCha McMillan who sometimes helped with the delivery route from his bicycle that he had won selling subscriptions. That day he wanted to buy a classified to try and give away a free, part-Labrador retriever puppy. I saved him the expense of a classified.

We loaded Buster the new puppy and ourselves into the Pinto and headed toward Jimmy's folks' home in Shawmut, Alabama. While in Alabama, we hoped to convince Millard, the generous editor, to co-sign for a bank loan to keep The Sun afloat. That was the extent of our plan: ask Millard for more money.

The plan did not work. Millard had his own troubles, what with running the *Opelika-Auburn News* and publishing several other smaller area newspapers. He simply couldn't commit to our request for a financial reprieve. And we were reluctant to stick our own necks any further in the financial guillotine; already we were several months behind in Pinto payments, and there were no guarantees subscriptions would pick up, or, more to the point, begin.

Editor Millard Grimes was and is a journalism hero. As his report-ers, we used to smile and call him the Columbo of Journalism because of his sometimes bumbling approach to our trade. He was easy to underestimate, and many did. Millard often appeared unfocused, even confused, but somehow, like Columbo, saved the day every time. He never hesitated to invest funds in the editorial side of the commercial product called a newspaper. When we approached him with a thick prospectus for starting the *St. Simons Sun*, he read it the same night. The next day, wearing a pink icing mustache from a cupcake celebrating the birthday of one of the paste-up women in the back shop, Millard nonchalantly wrote a check for $10,000 and handed it over to two twenty-something newspaper novices. I still lacked a college degree; Jimmy had his diploma and had been working for Millard for about a year. But Mister Grimes, as we always called him, saw our hunger and ambition and also a long-shot business opportunity to establish a real newspaper in a growing area.

"I've always liked that place," he said casually of St. Simons. Then he told us to stop by his Phenix City, Alabama, newspaper on our way down to the island and pick up some antique type-setting equipment, cantankerous machines called Justowriters, already dinosaurs in 1975.

Millard Grimes then proceeded to let us alone to sink or swim off the Georgia coast, visiting only once during the weeks we kept the newspaper alive. I remember taking him out to eat—at The Inward Point, of course. He made few suggestions, paid us compliments, and never questioned where the money went. I think he knew. He gave us permission to reprint his *Opelika-Auburn News* political column, which often veered into Georgia politics that he understood from having worked as editor in Columbus, Georgia.

I think in some unspoken ways we were relieved the week after Christmas when Millard told us he'd spent all the company money he could on *The Sun*. At best we felt ambivalence about not having to return to starve to death while putting in eighty or more hours a week for no money.

After that week of worried holiday, we returned to the island, defeated and embarrassed. All of our grand pronouncements about intending to stay forever had been premature, to say the least. Our apartment lease wasn't even up.

We packed a U-Haul with our few possessions, including the old Justowriters that had proved next to worthless. We cleaned up and closed down the office, no small task given the way we'd used the two rooms for everything from a business office to a place to roll papers in preparation for throwing. An old VW van we had bought at some point to help with deliveries wouldn't crank; we left it dead in the apartment parking lot. Jimmy would take a Greyhound down later to fix and retrieve it. We crossed back over the causeway to the mainland chastened and wiser.

The last issue of *The Sun* had been a hefty ten pages, including a full-page house ad begging for subscriptions. There was a story about Christmas mail declining slightly during the holiday season, a Millard Grimes political column, a list of Christmas church services, a rock band review and a small boxed item with the headline: *How about a holiday? After publishing Thanksgiving Day and Christmas, the staff of the* St. Simons Sun *is ready for a holiday. In order to have one,* The Sun *will not be published this coming week. The next* Sun *will be issued Thursday, Jan. 8. Watch for IT!*

Maybe some are still watching.

The most prescient thing about the issue was a front page, below-the-fold photograph captioned "Winter Sun." Jimmy took the photo of the setting sun, and I probably wrote the caption. Not my proudest moment. It said:

> The beautiful St. Simons sunsets like this one will be coming later and later each day now until June. The first day of winter, the shortest day of the year, came Monday. The Sun (sic) begins its northward trek now, and those folks at the north poll (sic) have only three months until morning . . .

My god, we were young and tired. That's my only defense.

# 9

# Frozen Toilets, Fledgling Talent

We moved out of the Monroeville, Alabama, mansion and into a cheap motel the day the water in the toilet bowls froze. As beautiful as the stone hacienda with its red tile roof was, it wasn't worth the pain. The house was huge and rambling, with fireplaces you could walk into standing upright. But we could afford to warm only the kitchen with a propane heater. You would have had to be as rich as the absentee owner to heat the entire house. By the time January rolled around with record lows, I was ready to find saner if less glamorous housing.

Besides, living there had tortured me, knowing for certain I'd never own the amazing house, not if I lived to be a thousand and worth a million. Owning was one thing. Renting another. We paid only $200 a month, minus whatever we spent on upkeep. We were billed as caretakers, though we hadn't the time or the resources to warrant the title. We mostly took care not to break anything expensive. But that was the deal with the absentee owner who came up from Mobile every now and then to check on her house. She was the daughter of the late lawyer named Hybart who had built the palatial home in the 1920s.

Thank goodness it didn't get frigid and unbearable until about a month after Christmas. Jimmy and I were given the gift of one wonderful holiday season in the mansion, which the whole town called the Hybart House. We had marched into the woods that surrounded it and cut our own tree. We had played carols on the old upright piano in the cavernous living room, mostly "Silver Bells" because it was one I could play and knew all the words to. We even had a Christmas party, inviting friends we had made at the *Monroe Journal*, the weekly newspaper where we'd taken jobs after the failure of the *St. Simons Sun*. I had candles burning in every giant window, and the end result was splendor on a shoestring. I could squint and pretend to be lady of the manor, some Carnegie or Vanderbilt, occasionally checking my reflection in a gilded mirror larger than most apartments I'd known.

Newspapers had nepotism policies then. Before the Gannett chain embraced the obvious incestuousness of the business and allowed couples to work in the same newsrooms, most dailies frowned on in-house marriages. If the inevitable romances happened, someone, usually the woman, had to quit.

So it had been hard to find a newspaper that would hire us both, especially since we had limited experience and one memorable failure on our resumes. The *Monroe Journal* was itself a family affair. Bill Stewart was owner and publisher, his son Steve the editor, and daughter-in-law Patrice the rest of the team. They appreciated our situation. And we worked cheap.

Jimmy and I divided the workload right down the middle. I typed up half the country correspondence that came in from Excel and Repton, Uriah and Frisco City, most of it scrawled in nearly indecipherable longhand; he did the rest. I typed up half the engagements and weddings, he did the rest. I wrote half the photo captions, he wrote half. We both covered city councils, trials, moonshine raids, bloody automobile accidents, planning commissions, church services, and beauty contests.

Monroeville was the home of both Harper Lee and Truman Capote. If you have to make a living slaving for The Man on a weekly newspaper, we could have chosen worse. The town's literary history made it interesting, and Steve Stewart was an amazingly good young editor. Steve and Patrice became our friends as well as our bosses, and we all shared the same liberal political leanings.

It was an exciting news era. Jimmy Carter was the Democratic nominee for president, Swine flu scared the common sense out of the nation and the country prepared to celebrate its bicentennial. We were learning the essentials of good journalism, things like how to coax information from secretive public officials and how to spell "boutonniere" and "cummerbund." I sat through many an Excel city council meeting, marveling at the quick comedown from part-owner and co-editor of my own weekly in paradise to lowly rural reporter.

The night the councilmen, and they were all men then, debated whether to pay the police chief overtime to clean the dirt dauber nests off the town siren, I felt my lofty journalism plans slipping away. But, needing the job, I went back and fashioned a lead for a story about thin budgets and persistent dirt daubers, and it wasn't half bad if I say so myself.

Our big dreams were on hold in that little town, but somehow living in the Hybart House and having smart colleagues made that bearable. We hosted parties, one of them forced outside and held by lantern light when we discovered, minutes before the party was set to begin, that the power company had remembered a bill we had forgotten. We got away with it until someone asked where the bathroom was.

Before the Carter election victory in November 1976, we invited every Democrat, black and white, in Monroe County—not a big crowd—to a pre-election planning meeting at the big house. Jimmy and I took the money we'd been saving for a washing machine and bought a full-page advertisement in our own newspaper supporting Carter. It wasn't the most professional move either of us ever made, but I still feel good about it. Monroe County, mostly because of its black population, narrowly went for Carter; Alabama narrowly went for Carter; the South narrowly went for Carter. Carter won.

We took personal interest in that presidential election with some cause. Millard Grimes had driven Jimmy and me to Atlanta in 1974, the night Carter announced to a incredulous and small crowd that he planned to run for president. I wrote the story, Jimmy took the photographs, and Millard, of course, got a column out of the goings-on that night. We were the only out-of-state newspaper to bother with coverage. After seeing the campaign in its infancy, I guess we felt destined to raise the child.

Mostly, though, the *Journal* was about local news. And local news ran the gamut. I wrote a feature on a woman and her prize zinnias. The local civil rights activist, Ezra Cunningham, was a familiar subject. We shot photographs of more big snakes and little beauties than we had ever thought possible.

"I want to report a cotton bloom," a booming voice said over the telephone one day when Jimmy happened to answer.

"Yes?" he said.

"Am I the first?" the reader asked.

"The first what?" a confused Jimmy responded.

"If I'm the first cotton bloom, don't you want to come take a picture?"

"I don't believe we'd be interested in that," Jimmy said politely but with finality. You had to draw the line somewhere.

He recounted the conversation to Steve later, only to discover the *Journal* always made a really big deal of the first reported cotton bloom of the year. Jimmy always felt bad that the photographic honors of 1976 probably went to the *second* bloom in Monroe County.

They cut down Boo Radley's oak tree the year we lived in Monroeville. Its diseased limbs were falling around the heads of school children. It was one of the last authentic props in the town where Nelle Harper had learned it was a sin to kill a mockingbird. We never met the great lady. We would hear that Harper Lee had been in town, but only after the fact. We knew her sister, lawyer Alice Lee, who once gave Jimmy a ride home from a planning commission meeting.

We lived well on our modest salaries. In the interest of time, we usually ate lunch out at one of two restaurants—the Heigh-Ho and the Tally-Ho. Why restaurateurs in Monroeville had an Old English fetish was never clear to me.

We were young and yearned for entertainment. There was none. There was a movie theater in town, and in our boredom we saw every picture that came to town, including *Eat My Dust* with Ron Howard, the last show to play before the old building burned to the ground one night.

Many weekends we drove to the National Seashore near Pensacola, about a two-hour trip, to camp on the same sugary beaches I'd known as a child. We packed light and traveled cheap. Lying on the sand, looking up at a trillion stars, we found ourselves once again yearning to be something more than we were—currently half the staff of an Alabama weekly. We didn't want much. We only wanted fame and fortune from semi-marketable creative talent.

We might be in Monroeville still if it hadn't gotten so cold and miserable in January 1976. Even my imagination and bittersweet love for the unattainable mansion couldn't get past the unpleasant realities of living in one room, albeit the kitchen. When we were forced to the motel, I decided on the spot to go back to Auburn and finish the twenty hours of academic work I'd left hanging when we moved to St. Simons. The missing diploma had never worried me before. I rather heartlessly left Jimmy working in Monroeville while I rented a room from an Auburn girlfriend and enrolled for one last scholastic quarter. I needed to get my degree, I claimed, if only to pacify my parents who were still appalled that I'd left school before officially graduating. And I did that, two years after I was supposed to graduate. My 1977 graduation date makes me look younger in the alumnae news.

I think back now about the dozens of newspaper jobs I've had over the years. I don't think a single editor ever asked me about my journalism degree. Most were far more interested in the St. Simons experience. Turns out every newspaper hack who ever drew a breath dreamed of starting his own weekly. I've always been grateful we got past that universal desire early, if only to see it's a hell of a lot of work and not all it's cracked up to be. There's a journalistic corollary that few people on dailies would admit: the larger the newspaper, the easier your job.

Jimmy joined me from Monroeville quickly enough, knowing down deep I'd escaped for more than a few months. The twin cities of Auburn and Opelika seemed like real metropolises after Monroeville, and we happily settled in for several years, enjoying the night life and working at both the local newspapers and the university. University towns are great places to live, especially if you are young. Something's always going on, and entertainment is cheap and plentiful.

But then one day it came Jimmy's turn to bolt. He decided his ultimate ambition wasn't writing public relations copy for the School of Engineering, comfortable and lucrative as that situation was. He got out his neglected drawing pen, his one-ounce bottle of FW, non-clogging, waterproof, India ink, and a blank piece of paper and drew us into the future.

# 10

# Arlo and Arlo

The hitchhikers were young women, drenched and shaking themselves like wet puppies beneath an overpass in Jackson, Mississippi. It was a foggy, soggy Christmas day, for heaven's sake, and you'd have to have been colder than bagged ice in Alaska to pass them up on such a morning.

Besides, I picked up hitchhikers quite often back then, having discovered altruism sometimes led to a column, if nothing else a column about picking up hitchhikers. I pulled my Mustang right next to the duo and asked if they wanted a hot meal. We were about to have a big one. Jimmy always made his mother's stomp-down delicious cornbread dressing to go with the Christmas turkey, while I gladly assumed the gofer role. I'd been dispatched to the convenience store, the only thing open, for some missing ingredient, probably salt, which would be about the only thing a store open on Christmas day would have on its shelves.

"We really just need a ride to Vicksburg," one of the women said through a veil of water.

"Can't help you there, but I can give you something to eat, some dry clothes and bring you back here when the rain lets up," I said, all benevolence and light. It was Christmas, after all!

"OK," she shrugged.

"Bless her heart," I thought. She's too tired and weak to appreciate her luck.

We were living in an ugly, large, rambling rental house in South Jackson, with wall-to-wall and ugly carpets left over from its glory days, obviously in the 1960s. The house had tell-tale modish features like hot pink tile in one of the four bathrooms, tile that was both dated and cracked, and dark sheet paneling in a big cave of a den. In one room there was a blue-green rug that put you in mind of a pool table. But the house was easily spacious enough to accommodate four of us. Jimmy and me, when I was there, and a newspaper colleague, Curtis Coghlan, who worked at the *Jackson Daily News* where Jimmy had landed a job in 1979 as editorial cartoonist. Also splitting the rent was Steve Haffly, an affable musician whose day job was collecting payments due, usually long overdue, for a band instrument store.

We called it the Smurf House for an obvious reason—there were lots of males, or Smurfs, and only one female, or Smurfette. I was working for the Memphis newspaper, the *Commercial Appeal*, and I traveled a lot. But when I was home, the boarding house arrangement made for a lot of fun and cheap living. There was always someone in the mood to drink a beer, or watch an old episode of the *Andy Griffith Show*. We were all, in fact, charter members of the Otis Campbell Chapter of the Andy Griffith Show Rerun Watchers Association. Yes, Virginia, there is such a club. Dues cost one dollar annually; it was the only thing I had joined since high school.

There was a restaurant right across the street called Po' Folks, appropriately enough, and we often walked over en masse, waited for the call—"Smurf, party of four"—and ate something delicious, unhealthy, and cheap like red beans and rice. Rarely did we use the stove, which once had been a top-notch appliance. It mostly served as a bed for the community cat, Miss Kitty, who seemed to like the comforting feel of cold aluminum.

Curtis and Steve were with their families on that Christmas day when I picked up the hitchhikers, but we knew they'd be back that night to help eat leftovers. Jimmy never did anything halfway, anyhow. Whenever he went in the yard to cut the grass, you might find him an hour later building a fountain or patio instead. If I fussed, he said I lacked vision. I probably did.

The Christmas feast he was preparing would be more than enough for us and the two skinny strangers I was hauling home, and still leave lots for leftovers. Jimmy had shooed Miss Kitty off the stovetop early that morning and had been cooking away ever since.

Our unexpected guests were quiet, to say the least. It was an awkward meal, what with me trying to draw them out and failing spectacularly. I don't remember, but I probably had a column due. I was hoping they would have an interesting story about why they were standing under an interstate bridge on Christmas day. One of my all-time favorite column quotes had come from a hitchhiker. Joe Olczak was quoting a German man who had given him a lift one day and, Joe said, gave the best description of America he'd ever heard. "He said this country was great because the matches and maps are free at service stations. How about that, heh? The matches and maps here are free."

Maybe that's what is wrong with the country now. Nothing is free at a today's service stations, including matches and maps. They even charge for air.

Pearls of wisdom were not exactly dropping from the tight lips of the Christmas hitchhikers. I remember only one conversational contribution the women made, the apparent leader speaking for them both.

"We never had dressing made like this," she said, pushing her dish away and lighting a cigarette. "It's not real good."

Jimmy rolled his eyes behind their backs as he went to get more rolls. The wayfaring women didn't eat enough to feed winter birds, and kept looking at us suspiciously like we might be dangerous ax murderers trying to lure them into white slavery with cranberry sauce and bad cornbread dressing. My holiday bonhomie was fading fast. I quickly ransacked my closet and gave the women a couple of dry jogging suits and took them back to their hitchhiking station located conveniently near a truck stop. At least the rain had stopped. Later, when I got home, Jimmy reminded me of that wisest of sayings: no good deed goes unpunished.

The Smurf House usually wasn't lacking for good conversation and plenty of cheerful noise even when it wasn't Christmas. On the contrary. It was a lowbrow literary salon. Steve was often found banging out a Jimmy Buffett song on his old piano, especially "A Pirate Looks at Forty," a song he really identified with.

*"Made enough money to buy Miami, but pissed it away so fast . . .*

Newspaper friends often would gather for impromptu meals, mostly restaurant take-outs eaten out of styrofoam boxes or greasy sacks. And you don't get reporters together without hearing great political gossip and partly informed, at least, opinions on absolutely everything. There was a steady stream of oddball traffic through that old suburban house, and I soon decided that Smurf living beat the hell out of any conventional arrangement. Every once in a while I'd worry that maybe there was something unhealthy about having Curtis along for our tenth wedding anniversary dinner, or always having to step over sleeping stragglers on the floor on your way to the bathroom at night, but, at that point in my life, I wouldn't have had it any other way.

Steve and Curtis both were single. Curtis was pretty much a typical newspaper workaholic, but Steve found the time between collections calls to date a lot and brought home plenty of interesting women. One night for a party at the house he arrived with twin sisters, both nurses. I never did figure out how that happened, but we never stopped kidding him about his suave "playboy" moves.

"Remember the twins," became our equivalent of "Remember the Alamo."

We all spent a lot of weekends on water, either driving down to the Mississippi Gulf Coast to catch a ferry out to Ship Island, or closer by on the Barnett Reservoir. That pretty lake was unfortunately named for Ross Barnett, the old segregationist governor who pretty much single-handedly incited the 1962 Ole Miss riots. Jimmy loved sailing, and with my journalism prize money— I won the 1983 national Ernie Pyle Award for feature writing—we managed to buy a sailboat we named, aptly enough, *The Ernie Pyle*.

I loved my job. Desperate to be back in the newspaper business, I had begun working for the Memphis newspaper's bureau system, which meant a commuting marriage. When Jimmy's long-shot bid to become an editorial cartoonist actually worked, I was odd journalist out. I was told by the *Jackson Daily News* and its sister paper, the *Clarion-Ledger*, that couples could not be hired by the same newspaper company. (Never mind it was then a family newspaper operation. What was good for the chiefs wasn't necessarily good for the Indians.) Out of necessity, I had, for a year, taken a writing job at the Mississippi Research and Development Center, which proved the most miserable professional year of my life. And, to that date, the most lucrative. But I hated the deliberate, academic pace of the center, which did some good things but ever so slowly. My boss would give me a news release assignment, and I'd have it back to her in ten minutes.

"Oh?" she would say, looking irritated. "I meant for you to work on that all this week."

Ever so often, I would write to the Memphis editors and beg the *Commercial Appeal* to give me a job. They, too, had a litany of reasons why it would not work out. Each time I chose a new editor to approach, hoping someone would take pity and hire me.

"You'd be miserable with your husband in Jackson and you in Memphis," the city editor said in a letter I kept. But with him I sensed an opening. When I persisted and he realized how passionately determined I was to take a big pay cut and work long hours away from my own home, he hired me for a bureau job in the Mississippi Delta town of Greenville. It was just before Christmas, 1980.

It meant, of course, that Jimmy and I had to pay rent in two places and would see one another only on weekends. Jimmy was not wild about the arrangement, but he had seen me truly miserable when forced out of the newspaper business. During our first year in Jackson, I couldn't even watch *Lou Grant* without feeling left out and tormented. Being a good friend as well as my husband, Jimmy agreed to the arrangement.

I was ecstatic to be reporting again. I loved the windowless office in the old May Building in downtown Greenville where countless bureau reporters before me had scribbled hundreds of telephone numbers on the wall. The office was about the size of a telephone booth, appropriately enough, only without the view. The city fire marshal came by every now and again to issue a warning about the old newspapers piled to the ceiling, but each bureau person in turn ignored him. It was perfect.

I loved the Delta itself, a lush land of contrast—extreme poverty and obscene wealth, ignorance and genius, black and white and Chinese communities. Nelson Street with its clubs and blues remained, at that time, what Beale Street in Memphis used to be and now only pretends to be. There were hot tamale stands and Doe's Eat House and its legendary steaks. There was a Chinese meat market with a butcher who fashioned raw meat sculptures from pork and beef.

Most of all, I loved the job. With eight or ten counties to mine for stories each day, there was never a slow day. You could always count on a murder trial, or a crop duster crash, or a thorny issue to explore in Greenville's federal courthouse where Judge William Keady presided. Keady was a big man, with white hair, and he wore saddle oxfords under his federal robes. He had a booming voice and a that's-settled delivery that sounded just like Old Testament God. Because of an ace reporter named Jim Young who once covered his court, Judge Keady loved the *Commercial Appeal* and gave us access and scoops.

Notorious Parchman Prison was part of my beat, and I toured that old working farm more than once. It was another world, where you didn't want to live. But the best concert I ever heard, bar none, was when B. B. King brought his guitar Lucille to the Parchman rodeo arena and gave a heavily guarded concert for the prisoners. It was hotter than a stewpot in the center of that arena, and every now and then the prisoners would raise such a righteous ruckus the guards would wave their guns for intimidation value. It didn't work. B. B. King was from just down the road, the steamy Delta burg of Indianola, and he no doubt recognized, as we all should, that but for a twist of fate he might be living the blues instead of singing them.

I often did my driving and reporting during the day, and then wrote into the night. That left me free to begin the process all over again the next morning. I rented a cobbled-on, narrow back room of an organ teacher's house on Greenville's funky Eureka Street. Often, late at night, after she'd had a vitamin shot that gave her excess energy, my landlord would be playing "Lady of Spain" or some other standard at top volume on the organ while I typed my next day's story. I always thought living there might have made my prose livelier.

All in all, it was heaven. Never, before or since, have I felt so compelled to write, so interested in every aspect of the days and nights. It's no mystery to me why Mississippi produced so many writers and musicians and artists. The raw material is in Mississippi. Characters are lousy on the ground. Racial tension is a truck crop. Music is a laxative. The stark beauty with each sunset is an artistic charge.

I met and wrote about Delta friends like John Odis, a shoeshine man who popped his rag right outside the front door of the May Building. He would ride the building's elevator with a mess of fish beaded on a stringer, stopping at each floor to show us occupants his pungent trophies.

His death in 1983, two years after I'd left that town, seemed to me to personify everything right and wrong between the races in Mississippi. They wouldn't dig John Odis's grave until the cash was in hand. So the weary old black man was buried weeks later, only after a group of white lawyers raised $165 for a country cemetery plot. Odis already had paid for his cheap wooden box through a small burial policy.

When Odis showed up in Greenville in 1970, Robert May let him erect his shoeshine business outside the front door of the downtown office building. May termed it a "nuisance," what with Odis's messy tobacco habit and the sizable crowds the personable shoeshine man attracted.

The last year of his life had begun badly. Odis had been mugged by hoodlums and had his Social Security check stolen a couple of times. His pride and joy, an outboard motor he regularly affixed to rented boats, had been stolen. Even his tackle box, filled with second-hand lures, was taken from him.

Odis, who had been a white doctor's chauffeur and a shoeshine man, sometimes was ridiculed by other blacks for his subservient lifestyle. And he was a master of shuck and jive. But in his scrappy way, he made his own living even with a laundry list of ailments. His white friends proved genuine, and in the end they were the ones who buried him. But then, he was satisfied with a borrowed piece of the white man's sidewalk.

The Delta had an anachronistic quality that I loved and resented, and it was full of John Odises, juicy leftovers from the fiction of Faulkner and Flannery O'Connor. The Delta had soul in abundance. I often was the only white person at black mass meetings, or blues funerals, or honkytonks. Once I covered a reception for Washington, D.C., Mayor Marion Barry in his hometown of Itta Bena. At the time I had a dark tan but irreconcilable blue eyes. "You aren't Caucasian. What race are you?" someone asked.

Best of all, the Greenville job put me back in the reporting business I'd so sorely missed. I'd never seriously wanted to be anything but a newspaper reporter, if you didn't count my brief childhood ambition to become a veterinarian. I still don't, really. It's a sad thing in life that I have outlasted newspapers, or most of them. I was happiest striking out in an old car with cheap gas and a reporter's notebook, not knowing exactly what I might find or even where I was going. No two days were alike, except in the way they ended at my desk with the tough but gratifying challenge of stringing words and facts together in a pleasing way.

My sweet Grannie was buried in south Georgia the same week I started that dream job in Greenville. I hadn't even had time to move into my one-room apartment yet, but was living in a cheap motel on the edge of town. I didn't go back to Colquitt for the funeral, rationalizing that Grannie never liked for me to miss work on her behalf, and that she'd never know I had not made it. Pop already was dead, and my mother had my father and her siblings for support.

The December day of Grannie's funeral it was difficult to concentrate. I tried extra hard to land a story on the front page in her honor. The story didn't make front page. Bureau stories rarely did, unless they involved multiple corpses. But she would have smiled to see me so happy again, thrust among and writing about luckless people like the ones she always helped. The gypsies that camped in her back pasture knew to knock on her door for food. The hoboes who passed through town knew about her, too. I inherited blue eyes and a soft heart from my grandmother, and hers was the unqualified love that kept me sane. I still miss her.

I believe it was that happy year in Greenville when I learned the most valuable writing lesson ever. The assignment was a boring one, a two-bit city election in the neighboring community of Leland. I remember rifling the files to see how the last bureau reporter had covered the last Leland city election; I meant to copy his approach.

I drove over to Leland, hoping to see something interesting to jog a thought. What I saw were button-downed, young, clean-cut candidates still handing out their campaign literature near the polling place. On the drive back to Greenville, something in me rebelled against fill-in-the-blank, do-it-as-it-is-always-done, wire service-style news writing. *I could make this halfway interesting,* I thought.

My lead surprised even me. *It looked like a Jaycee convention turned loose early,* I wrote.

To their credit, Memphis editors loved the creative initiative and put the little piece on page one. They created a monster. After that day, I wrote to please myself, respecting the rules of grammar and good journalism, but not the idea that some stories are simply throwaway material and don't merit great care with the writing. Every story has front-page potential, I decided, and my new approach brought big dividends. Not every story I wrote made page one, but a lot of unlikely ones did. I was learning so much on this job that every day was a stunning revelation. I was insatiably hot for newspaper journalism.

It was with heavy heart that I gave notice about a year later to take a job with United Press International in Jackson, the underdog wire service in our state and in the nation. I took the job because I thought it best to try and live under one roof with my husband—for any number of reasons. First, there was the economics of a commuting marriage. It was a strain. Then, of course, there was the toll the long absences took on our marriage. That veteran city editor had known what he was talking about.

And, maybe most important of all, it was almost Christmas.

Wire service work was okay, but the freedom that a reporting job usually affords was completely missing. In the small Jackson bureau, we mostly conducted telephone interviews, dozens of them a day. Each story had to be written three ways, once for the morning newspapers, another version for the afternoon papers, and a third for broadcast subscribers. There wasn't much time left for feature-writing, my forte. We routinely did weather reports, livestock and chicken market updates, sports teasers for half a dozen colleges, and copious rewrites from our subscribers' newspapers. I learned to write quickly.

"Get them chickens!" Billy James, the colorful morning man, would holler as I walked through the door to relieve him about noon each day. That command meant to phone a certain number for the information needed for the poultry report.

It wasn't glamorous journalism, that's for sure, and a large percentage of time was spent pacifying insatiable radio managers who were never happy with the rip-and-read copy that clicked from our heads and hands into their stations. Some of the faceless tyrants on the telephone were astounded to reach a female voice that said in her most authoritative wire service voice, "Johnson, UPI."

"Let me speak to a real reporter," one station manager said.

I stayed only long enough for the UPI job to look respectable on my resume, but was delighted when a *Commercial Appeal* editor telephoned one day and said there was another bureau opening, this one in Mississippi's Tupelo. Once again I packed my bags. I stayed on shady Green Street, where Elvis's family once had lived. Truth is, Elvis Presley's poor and struggling folks lived on almost every street in Tupelo at one time or another. But it sure sounded cool to claim you lived on Elvis's old street, which I did at every opportunity.

Tupelo wasn't as rich—in any sense—as the Delta, but I had fun on the job there, too. There was the usual complement of Mississippi small-town characters. A kind retired policeman named Eldridge Dalee brought me Almond Joy bars and boiled eggs with Magic Marker inscriptions—"Proud of You," an egg might say. He left them outside the office door each morning, also marking the time on the egg. He made most of his deliveries around 4 A.M.

I sometimes slept on the screened sleeping porch of a house that had belonged to the parents of a UPI buddy, Andy Reese. Andy had inherited the place and let me use it for the cost of utilities. That helped some of the economic strain Jimmy and I had been feeling.

In Greenville I had pretty much been paying to work.

There was a fly in the ointment, however. There always is. The nagging insecurities I had battled since childhood lingered, and did not make for a smooth marriage. I often was jealous, unreasonably so, and struggled with a baseless fear that Jimmy would someday leave me. Whenever he so much as looked at a pretty woman, I'd make life miserable for him and counter with a flirtation of my own. Our marriage seemed perfect to friends, so free-wheeling and modern, but they weren't there for the dark nights of the soul-sapping arguments caused mostly by my emotional outbursts and immaturity.

Jimmy's work, too, was fettered by an ultra-conservative old editor named Jimmy Ward. Ward had become well known beyond the region for his frequent contributions to the Paul Harvey radio show. Harvey often referred to "Jackson's Jimmy Ward," the same Neanderthal that Jimmy had to get his editorial cartoons past. Despite the handicap, Jimmy's work was part of a winning Pulitzer package and individually he won the Robert Kennedy award for progressive and socially conscious journalism.

Jackson's Jimmy Ward and my Jimmy eventually, inevitably, reached an impasse. Jimmy quit cartooning and worked the copy desk, a move that might have been too humbling for many egos, but one he made graciously to help keep paying the rent. The rents. In his free time he started trying to develop a cartoon strip, another long-shot ambition that I encouraged. Even when we were battling about everything else, Jimmy and I supported one another professionally. After receiving lukewarm encouragement from United Media Syndicate, Jimmy left the copy desk and devoted full time for a year to the development of *Arlo and Janis*, a strip about—you guessed it—a liberal and young married couple with a son named for Eugene McCarthy. Arlo harkened to Arlo Guthrie and Janis to Janis Joplin. After *Arlo and Janis* became a newspaper fixture, fans would often ask about the son. "Since you don't have children, how does Jimmy know so much about them?" the question usually went.

"I was a child once," Jimmy would say.

Fans forever and falsely assumed that the strip was strictly autobiographical because Arlo looked so much like Jimmy and Janis like me. Arlo was dreamy and impractical, which certainly fit. But Janis was the practical one, bringing Arlo to earth when he wanted to buy a sailboat instead of pay the power bill, or insisting the two of them eat sensibly and walk to stay physically fit. Except for the physical resemblance, I was nothing like Janis. I was another Arlo, perhaps more Arlo-esque than even Jimmy himself. I was a serious romantic, never taking the straight route or the obvious choice. I've thought through the years how good this arrangement was for us—at least in our jobs. What other husband would have encouraged his wife to commute for a poor-paying job when it meant long separations and doubling the rent? What other wife would have paid all the bills while her husband tried to sell a comic strip? What other couple would have struck out to a resort island with antique type-setting equipment to try and start a weekly newspaper?

If the comic strip had been strictly autobiographical, it would have been called Arlo and Arlo. We fed one another's fantasies and came of age professionally together. I've never regretted a single moment I spent with Jimmy.

A wonderful editor named Sarah Gillespie eventually flew from New York and visited the Smurf House, giving syndication guidance to Jimmy and bringing along a syndicate contract for him to sign. I never knew if Sarah realized she was conducting business in a house named for Belgian cartoon characters and fueled by beer and love. How appropriate. Sarah, it turned out, also was the editor for Charles Schulz and *Peanuts*.

With the sale of the strip, finally, we were free to move from Jackson to anywhere within the *Commercial Appeal* circulation area. We headed north, to a resort lake created on the Tennessee River by the Tennessee Valley Authority. Pickwick Lake had everything. Adirondack-looking cabins, proximity to Memphis, solitude for writing and drawing, and reasonably affordable (this has since changed) waterfront property. We bought three acres and a cabin on a bluff overlooking Pickwick and with a view of three states: Tennessee, Mississippi, and Alabama. I could drive less than twenty miles and have column datelines in all three states. The location had it all, slothful Southern personality and crisp New England looks. In the fall and winter, when the day-trippers from Memphis were back in school and at work, we had this world to ourselves, or so it seemed. I'd sit on the bluff and declare to anyone who'd listen that I was never leaving this idyllic spot, not ever, ever, ever.

The Smurf House concept moved with us. Curtis was reassigned by Gannett as an editor in Jackson, Tennessee, and he was a frequent weekend visitor, still wearing his worried work look and pressed, button-downed shirts. Steve, the freer spirit, had, by now, met the love of his life, another young musician named Cindy, and the two of them actually moved in with us while finagling to buy their own Pickwick cabin. They soon would find jobs in the area as band teachers. Steve's brother Dave, by now a cherished member of our group, a bona fide Smurf with all the benefits and perks that entailed, lived and worked in nearby Florence, Alabama, and came over to the lake every week-end. A food service manager for a college, Dave was as handy in the kitchen as big spoons. He wore an old parson's hat that looked like the one the character Will B. Dunn wore in Doug Marlette's comic strip *Kudzu* and did a dead-on Jim Jones impersonation while acting as official bartender.

"Come my children, drink the poison."

Our second year on the happy bluff we had what we called, naturally, Smurf Christmas. The large, live tree was decorated with blue lights and Smurf action figures. We got the official, duty-bound, family stuff out of the way first, then celebrated in this whimsical, cartoonish atmosphere we'd proudly created. So what if we were thirty-something adults; we still knew how to have nonsensical fun. Plus, nobody yet had children. Everyone gave everyone presents. No frugal name-drawing for the Smurfs. A couple of Pickwick Lake outsiders we'd accepted into our fold were included. We had "kidnapped" them from their beds late one night, blindfolded them, and led them through an elaborate initiation ceremony with the stereo playing "Am I Blue?"

That year we even had a second lighted Christmas tree on the gazebo perched on the bluff for the passing barges to see. It hurt me to think that anybody was having a blue Christmas, except, of course, in the Smurf sense. We thought of everything, and Christmas was the best it had been since Ted could talk. For the first time in our married lives, against incredible odds, we had the work we'd dreamed about so long ago in the student newspaper office. I was a newspaper columnist for a large daily and Scripps Howard News Service. Jimmy had sold a comic strip. We had bought our dream home on a picturesque lake and were surrounded by good friends and all the right enemies.

So, quite naturally, always my own worst enemy, I threw a rock at it all.

# 11

# Fishtrap Hollow

I t was the giant old cedar at the end of the long drive that sold me. The tree was, in fact, all I paid much attention to the day the friendly real estate salesman obligingly drove me straight to what I'd asked to see: "a remote cabin with a few acres."

There were more than a few acres, actually, certainly more than I'd envisioned. There were 110 to be exact. The house was no great shakes, an amateurishly constructed country home from the 1950s that had been shrink-wrapped for resale with cardboard-looking siding that hid both asbestos and character. As was the style in the 1950s, the small floor space had been subdivided into many rooms, including a useless hallway, three bedrooms and a bathroom so small you could sit on the toilet, lean over the lavatory, and brush your teeth.

It was, as ordered, remote. And nobody had lived there for some time. The grass was shoulder-high. As I sat on the concrete steps the first night with a personal-sized picnic spread on my new oven's broiler pan, a black snake raced across my feet. I squealed. Like a girl. I wondered what I'd gotten myself into. A major home renovation project? Farming? A divorce? I'd left the most beautiful spot on the lake and a creative and kind man to land here near Hooterville on a *Green Acres* home site.

A hedge of privet outlined the front yard, separating it superficially from the unruly pasture that hadn't seen a cow in a coon's age. Beneath the privet were old and mud-filled soda bottles, juice and jelly jars, rubber hoses, car parts, smashed baseball caps, broken furniture and, yes, an old kitchen sink. Bedsprings, several sets, littered the yard. Every piece of metal I picked up to haul to the landfill was hiding a poisonous snake.

Even so, the place had its charms, including a spring-fed branch that zigzagged through the property like a scar on an ample belly. It would provide my drinking water for the first five years in the hollow. When I'd leave on some newspaper assignment for more than a few days, sand would collect in the pipe that brought the water from the spring through the branch and to the little pump house. I'd usually arrive home after dark, knowing there was a fifty-fifty chance there would be no water. I had a pressurized air tank I carried, along with a flashlight, to a spot in the creek where the pipe was coupled with a connector valve. I'd uncouple the pipe and blow air in both directions.

One night, nothing worked. I finally looked through the connecting valve with one eye like a sailor and saw only darkness. So I put my mouth to one end of the valve and blew. A dead and bloated salamander popped out of the other end, and I soon had running water.

Despite such gory setbacks, I had lived with Jimmy and his vision thing long enough to see potential. Even the sad little house had promise. Tradesman after tradesman advised me to "Tear it down," always reminding me of the Cary Grant movie *Mr. Blandings Builds His Dream House*. But, unlike Mr. Blandings, I refused to give up on the old house. I have a stubborn streak the size of Kansas. The house had a certain fairytale quality, I thought, the suggestion in its proportions that seven dwarves might appear out the undersized door with shovels and picks in hand. *Heigh ho. Heigh ho.* There had to be something here worth saving.

And one night, while sitting on the porch, I looked across to the hayfield and saw lights. Lots of lights. It was as if a movie set of New York City had been transported to the dark old Mississippi hollow. I walked toward the light, like a zombie in a movie, moving down the driveway toward my mailbox on its crooked cedar post.

I finally realized I was seeing lightning bugs, millions of them, blinking their love in flickering installments of yellow and green, lighting up the acreage like a convention hall. It was, aside from the California redwoods, the most beautiful natural sight I'd ever seen. And it was at that moment I let go of my grief for the house on the bluff, that dramatic vantage that people now pay millions for but that Jimmy and I had managed practically to steal. I wasn't through grieving the marriage, but I was done with the place. I had, at least, found a new home.

I've spent many hours of my life trying to decide exactly how I emotionally made the lover's leap to Fishtrap Hollow, my name for the new place. Everyone in nearby Iuka, Mississippi, called it, with reason, the Old Red Brown place. Red Brown built the house, and once a man has hammered nails and planks he deserves to keep the title. I used, and use, Fishtrap Hollow as a dateline to make the location of my home vague in newsprint. You'd be surprised how many strangers will decide you'd like nothing more than to spend your weekend listening to them talk. I chose the "fishtrap" part because there once was an old wooden fishtrap on a Bear Creek cove near here, and I found the concept of tricking fish into a trap quite fascinating. Cruel, perhaps, but fascinating.

I was here and meant to make the best of it. I mowed and mopped, planted and plotted, all the while grieving. Best I can figure, living with Jimmy was just too easy for someone determined to make her life hard. I didn't trust the assurances he gave again and again that he would not leave me. "Sure you will," I told myself. And to nip that *GWTW* scenario in the bud, I did the most illogical logical thing I could think of. I left him.

Jimmy had faults, but overall he was a kind, intelligent, and tolerant husband. I don't know why I couldn't be content with that arrangement, or at least wait and see if the "inevitable" leave-taking actually would happen. He had never given the slightest indication that it would. Basically, this inability to allow myself to be loved was mired in the muddle that is childhood. All of us are marked by our parents for good and for bad. It's not an excuse, just an observation. I didn't trust real love. Before I lapse into psycho-babble—or what my father used to call "nickel-assed psychology"—I'll sum it up this way: It happened. I left. I've been sorry. I've been glad. I've been lonely. I've found love. It happened. Things do.

Every day in small-town America couples celebrate their fiftieth wedding anniversaries in Baptist church basements with the pomp and circumstance of a royal wedding. That goal—making it to the fiftieth wedding anniversary—seems to encase some marriages like shrink-wrap around a sausage. It's a worthy goal, evidently an end unto itself. That party, to some, is worth all the trouble of fifty years of living with someone you either love to pieces or would like to hack to pieces. I'm sure both kinds of marriages make it to the Baptist church basement. I just never could envision it for myself. Maybe, like Jimmy said, I simply had no vision.

What I did have was a new friend, chosen carefully from our available acquaintances for the worst possible match. He was twenty years my senior, a functioning alcoholic, politically conservative, divorced twice with a boy child by each ill-fated marriage, clinically depressed, scornful of psychiatry, somewhat of a lady's man or at least looked like one for—did I mention?—he was drop-dead gorgeous. There were so many red flags I might as well have been at a Nebraska football game. Still, I jumped into the relationship with at least one foot. The other was noticeably dragging. I was so burdened with guilt and all its attendant depression that I spent many days driving myself the twenty-odd miles between my old home on the bluff and my new home in the hollow. But when nightfall came, I usually was in the company of the most controlling and determined, albeit charming, man I'd ever known.

His name was Barry. He was a lawyer like his father before him. The two had, in fact, practiced together for several years. Unlike many lawyers, Barry didn't have an ounce of greed in him. At least not greed for money. He seemed, in fact, to have an aversion to normal lawyer's fees. He would work a friend's divorce for a new shirt, waive his fee altogether for any relative or former in-law—and there were a lot of those—close a house deal for a meal, shut down his own office to go hunting or fishing with a friend. I admired all that about him. By all indications, he loved his two sons more than life itself. And he could make a party of any gathering, a festival out of any meal.

We argued incessantly. I'm not sure why, but we did. If Barry said he liked leather sofas, I'd immediately abhor them. If I found Bob Dylan's music enchanting, he'd find Dylan tone-deaf and disgusting. Jimmy and I had agreed on so many fundamentals that this new adversarial relationship was both an exciting challenge and a substantial bother. It may be true what they say about opposites attracting, but I think it was more a matter of opposites wearing one another down. Barry, for instance, eventually learned to like, or at least pretend to like, the primitive pieces I found charming and used to decorate my new house on the cheap. I was "shabby chic" before "shabby chic" was cool. And I eventually agreed that if you loved to eat doves, you probably shouldn't vehemently oppose a dove hunt. I never told him about all the turtles and sparrows I'd offed back in my pellet gun days.

On good days, we made light of our differences. He might, as a joke, stick a National Rifle Association sticker on my bumper. I'd counter with one from Amnesty International. He loved to talk, and at first I found fascinating his midnight ramblings about the many wrongs he'd endured from the opposite sex. He was a Mississippi Hamlet, a one-person show. Eventually I could tell from the way he held his rum glass which relationship and ex-wife he planned to expound on for the entire evening. I'd glaze over and settle in for the duration. The next morning, however, no matter how long the rant, he was at his office early, diligently fulfilling the "counselor" part of the "counselor at law" career he had chosen. And he was good at it, offering wisdom about everyone's relationships but his own. Those remained a complete mystery to him.

The first Christmas at my new farm in the hollow was a mixed success. I bought a Scotch pine growing from a big ball of dirt. I justified the considerable expense, reasoning it could be planted in the rather bare front yard after the holidays. I lovingly put it in a galvanized washtub that took up half the tiny living room and decorated it with plastic apples from Fred's Discount Store. On Christmas Eve, Barry's younger son and his girlfriend came and opened presents beneath my tree.

There was an achingly hollow feeling for all of us, I think, enduring that contrived merriment that made such a false and tinny sound. I was thinking about Smurf Christmas, the contentment and comfort of it all with a husband who loved me and with friends my own age. I'm sure Barry was thinking about the years when his son was little with both parents living together, over in a big brick ranch house with all the middle-class trimmings.

Jimmy and I would take longer to make our divorce official than some stay married. We were a poor man's Charles and Di. The painful purgatory of separation would last four years. It took a lot of nagging from our respective sweethearts before we would go through with the official papers, which, of course, Barry filed for free.

That first Christmas at the Mississippi farm, and several others that followed, Jimmy and I met up some time during the holidays and drove together to Alabama to see his ailing parents, whom we believed would literally die if they knew we'd broken up. On the long drive over, we spoke very few words, because at that point words always led to arguments. But once there, we were the happy couple, married for fourteen years, having a family holiday as was our tradition. We gave prize-worthy performances in the name of love, in the name of Christmas, in the struggle to find and do what is right.

# 12

# Refrigerator Babies

When you don't have children, maybe even if you do, well-meaning friends send you photographs of babies, their babies, in every stage of development from freshly hatched fetuses to fat, ugly toddlers. In the 1980s, when childbirth was still a personal possibility, I seemed to get more than my share of those photos. I got baby pictures from cousins, first and second, old high school buddies, near and far, column readers and other rank strangers.

I'd open an envelope, try to determine without reading whose "precious" baby might be in the photograph. Then I'd absentmindedly stick the picture to my refrigerator with tape or a magnet. It seemed wrong to throw something swaddled straight in the trash. Months later, sometimes days later, I would have forgotten who the baby might be, except the next likely cute candidate to fall off the refrigerator door to live with the dust bunnies beneath it.

I did not have children, none of my three siblings had children, and it looked like we might remain a barren bunch. Jimmy and I had discussed the possibility, but somehow I never felt old enough or wise enough to rear a child. In those days, I had to be careful to remember to feed the dog regularly. I was obsessed with my work, and, somehow, thank goodness, lacking the presumption I could guide another human being to an adulthood I had yet to reach myself.

Then one cold January morning in 1988, the phone rang twice within ten minutes, and life as I had known it changed forever. I sure didn't realize the momentousness at the time, or even suspect. It would be almost three years before the realization gripped me. The first phone call, however, did wake me.

"You're an aunt for the first time," my brother-in-law in Denver said. He was phoning on behalf of my older sister, JoAnne.

I said the usual congratulatory things, then rolled back over in bed.

The second call was my younger sister Sheila, sounding weak but calling for herself. "You're an aunt for the first time," she said.

"Not so fast," I replied from the fog of half-sleep. "We have to put a stopwatch to this."

My parents, who had about given up, had become grandparents twice over in a matter of minutes. I was now an aunt, as foreign a concept as if you'd suddenly anointed me a nuclear physicist. I vaguely had known both my sisters were pregnant but only when I bothered to remember. Our lives had gone in dramatically different directions in different places. I didn't talk a lot to either one. I had no idea nine months had passed since I'd heard the news about the pregnancies. Gestation goes fast for all but the pregnant. One sister had delivered two weeks early, the other two weeks late. I had no idea which was which.

Now those refrigerator babies came fast and furious. I could even tell these refrigerator babies apart. There were pictures of bald cherubs all over, as if Olan Mills had opened a concession in my house. Not content with still photography, both sisters invested in the video cameras that were ubiquitous in the 1980s. That, of course, meant hours of footage of babies drunkenly taking first steps, blowing spit bubbles, and regurgitating birthday cakes. It was a silly, disgusting business, I thought.

I made the trip to Alabama to my folks' house for the official debutante ball. Both sisters were bringing the babies for a Christmas visit. Aha, I thought. Two birds with one stone, er, trip. Quilt pallets were all over the floor, and you couldn't swing a cat without hitting some baby contraption. There were swings and beds and knapsacks. There were also Pampers. Lots and lots of those. I managed to get through an entire weekend without so much as holding an infant. Even if I had wanted to indulge, I would have had to wrestle one from my father.

On the other hand, I gave great gifts. I commissioned a German woman I knew to hand knit wool sweaters for each child. All of us in the family had to give the same thing to both babies lest one of the mothers find out you'd made a distinction and have a hissy fit. The hand-knit sweaters cost approximately the same as my Ford van. But I figured that was what an aunt did. She gave expensive, keepsake gifts and kept at least three framed photographs of each child in a prominent place in her house, rotating them depending on which sister was visiting.

Turns out, there's a little more to it. I began to realize this when the children reached two, then three, and became little people instead of mere maggots. I have never had the baby fetish that some women have. JoAnne will stop strangers pushing a buggy on the street and ask permission to chuck a chin. I once went with her to Paris and feared arrest because she accosted so many Parisian babies. Newborns just don't do it for me. But, turns out I'm a pushover for house-broken toddlers. Especially these particular toddlers, my blood kin, after all. They were the cutest children ever to fall down the fallopian tube. They said the most wonderful things, in the cutest baby talk ever uttered.

For the longest, my nephew Ben, JoAnne's child, could not pronounce "r." Which was especially endearing to me since it meant he said, "Aunt Wheta, may I wide with you?" and "Is that a choo-choo twain, Aunt Wheta?" It was too, too darling.

He was the neatest little thing, to boot, like a self-cleaning oven. Ben could play in mud and it wouldn't stick to him. He had these blond curls and amazingly pinch-able, cherubic cheeks and the disposition of an angel. He was too good to be true, which was convenient since my sister was a doctor and gone a lot.

Sheila's daughter, Chelsey, on the other hand, was not self-cleaning. You could dress her in a fresh outfit every five minutes and she'd look like Pigpen seconds later. She was precocious to Ben's innocent, and pretty demanding, too. She liked to be the center of attention, which she usually was.

"I'll be the teacher," she announced one night while rearranging my living room and wearing a chocolate milk-soaked nightgown. "You be one of those other people."

I studied on that a minute. "A student?" I asked.

"Yes, that's right," she said. "A bad one."

Chelsey liked to punish people, and I spent a whole lot of her first years in time-out. Only belatedly did I realize it was supposed to work the other way around.

Because the family made much of the children having the same birthday, a fierce competition grew up with them. Ben and Chelsey would fight over everything—a balloon, the right to sit next to me in the car, the name of the cat. The mothers, too, were competitive, worse than the children really, and compared every dimple and diaper.

Once, when they were about seven, both kids were at my house. I was trying to write. They burst into the room at the same time, both weeping, red and hot and mad.

"What's wrong?" I said, jumping up, truly alarmed. I thought maybe they'd been bitten by the same copperhead.

"She made fun of my school," Ben said through his hot tears.

"You made fun of mine first," wailed Chelsey.

"He said I make 'A's' because my school is full of hillbillies," Chelsey, the Kentucky native, explained.

"Well, you said my school is full of rich little snobs," Ben, from Denver, said between sobs.

I took a break from my writing to explain that the world has all kinds of people—including but not limited to hillbillies and snobs—and that most have merit, but worth isn't determined by what you own or how much money you have or whence you come. I quoted Kris Kristofferson's "Jesus Was a Capricorn," the verse about how *Everybody has to have somebody to look down on; if you can't find somebody else, then help yourself to me.*

I probably read them a chapter from Steinbeck's *Of Mice and Men* or suggested they watch the movie *Elephant Man.* I was in high dudgeon, holding forth on injustice and humility and the meek inheriting the earth. I was on such a roll I didn't notice they had gone.

I'm not sure when they left, bored out of their skulls. They were playing together, happy again, thinking that any insults they might hurl at one another had to be better than an adult lecture.

Many of my friends had children by now. Even the Smurfs had gone forth and multiplied. The carefree Steve and Cindy Haffly had a daughter, Carlin, named for their favorite comedian. Naming that child was their last frivolous act. Now they consorted mostly with other parents, with whom they had things in common, mainly children.

Curtis, always serious, had married by now and eventually would have two daughters. I never thought I'd quote that no-talent idiot Bocephus, but it fits: *All my rowdy friends have settled down.*

I was struck with the realization that the very thing I'd meant to avoid, that powerlessness you feel when it comes to children and their safety, had been thrust upon me nevertheless. By my sisters, those conniving wenches.

It has always struck me that to have children you almost *had* to be religious, else you were really out on a skinny limb alone. Childbirth not only affects female hormones; it must lube that part of the brain that wants, that needs, to count on something greater than ourselves. Someone to pray to for the safety of small and helpless creatures here on this earth because we had sex.

Chelsey and Ben would add to my life, give it a dimension I'd not known was possible. They would worry me, charm me, love me, make me proud. But they did not make me religious. Maybe it's because I did not give birth but only inserted myself into their lives when they were children. As much as I wanted to think Someone was watching over their every step—their dog-paddling in the deep end, their fevered foreheads, and their derring-do on skateboards and bikes—I knew, deep down, there was nobody Out There to back me up. When they were with me, I was in charge. I was responsible, or irresponsible, as the case might be. Not since I was twelve and feeling out of step with my Southern Baptist elders did I want so much to think there was a safety net for human mistakes and foibles. But all my life's training—the journalism, the hard knocks—made me know it wasn't so.

Some would call it existentialism, some would call it atheism. I would call it objectivity. Even though I loved these two babies with every breath in my body, I could not believe in a god who took the time to monitor my kin, or one who would decide willy-nilly which children would live, which would die, which would eat, which would go hungry, and which would prosper. Maybe if I'd actually given them life, I'd have to share that responsibility or be damned. But I did not. So I could not.

These refrigerator babies, like all the rest, were ultimately on their own.

# 13

# Why Don't You Like Me?

All my adult life, I've hidden in my work. Not behind it, but deep inside it, in those solitary moments at a keyboard when you and you alone know you're cooking. Nothing else matters. I've retreated to writing during the worst possible personal moments, the longest years. Writing has seen me through a divorce from a man I loved, the death of my dear second husband, and a ton of major crises and minor annoyances. Writing is something I can control. Life seems to be another matter.

One day in the late 1980s, after a long, typical, hellish night of arguing with Barry, my Memphis editor called with a column idea. That happened infrequently. It is hard to execute another's idea in a column, and a good editor knows that it is best to leave a columnist the hell alone. But when you have to produce four columns a week, a good idea from any source is gold. This was a good idea. The editor had read a short wire service story about the situation and recognized column potential.

In north Tennessee, right on the Kentucky border, a funeral home owner had been hauled off to jail for his own protection. Earlier that week he'd been charged with any number of fraudulent practices, including using and selling the same concrete burial vaults more than once. He'd also been caught rolling corpses in old carpet and reusing expensive caskets. He would sell the funeral goods, make a show at the burial, then go back under cover of night to dig up his merchandise. Now they'd hauled him to jail in another county to keep angry customers from killing him. People take burials seriously.

I ran to my car and broke speed limits getting to the county in question. There was a court-ordered exhumation scheduled at a certain cemetery to check for suspected irregularities, and I wanted to be there. Even before I got to the appointed place, the story about death came alive. As I got closer, each time I passed a country church, there were people roaming the cemeteries with probes in hand, checking relatives' graves. Was there a vault? Was there even a casket? Huddled graveside conferences were in progress everywhere, and the scene was both poignant and eerie.

I made it to the exhumation at the perfect time. Perfect, that is, if you're in the news business. The opening of the casket—presumably cradling somebody's mother, somebody's grandmother—couldn't have been more dramatic. Concerned kin huddled around in horror as the sheriff proceeded to show them that the pink satin lining that cushioned the corpse also hid empty Alpo dog food cans and other rubbish. The mortician had casually thrown his personal garbage into the casket. There was predictable weeping and outrage and disgust.

It was Halloween. It was a great column day. Such good material, in fact, that I wrote two columns back-to-back on the same subject, something I rarely did.

I suppose it sounds ghoulish to use that particular example as a memorable day in the life of a roving columnist. But I'm afraid it's a good one. Oh, there were a thousand brighter examples of journalistic coups: The old woman who ran a U.S. post office from her kitchen, selling stamps and envelopes while the pressure cooker rattled. The Tennessee couple who over the course of fifty years kept track of every penny they spent—every single penny, including the one in 1959 when her husband went downtown for a haircut and paid to weigh himself. And, there was the wonderful old grave digger in Paris, Tennessee, who still dug every grave by hand. He led me about the city cemetery and showed me where he had plugged former governors, and what plot held a certain used car salesman.

"Is there any difference in the way you feel when you bury them?" I asked. "Any difference between burying a governor and a car salesman?"

"No, ma'am," he said. "They all go 'bout six feet down."

Some days the planets align and you find the perfect, poignant story on what seems like the appropriate day. The Halloween and recycled casket column is a pure, if macabre, example. And the never-ending hunt for such rare and elusive columns kept me, believe it or not, sane.

My last full year living with Jimmy, I even collected a few of my early columns in a book that didn't sell many copies but helped my organizational skills and my ego. My first full year with Barry, I wrote the authorized biography of comic-strip genius Charles Schulz. Repeated trips to Santa Rosa, California, to "shadow" the famous cartoonist got me out of Mississippi and periodically away from a doomed relationship that was making me old fast. Charles Schulz, or "Sparky," as he asked me to call him, was a gentleman and a gentle man.

I first met Charles Schulz on Easter Sunday, 1988. He routinely booked rooms for his frequent out-of-town visitors in a motel lodge near his studio. I flew into San Francisco, rented a car and drove to the lodge. It being a Sunday, especially Easter Sunday, I didn't expect to meet the world-famous artist until the next day. A couple of hours after I arrived and had settled in with a book, the famous multimillionaire Sparky tapped on my door. He was holding an Easter basket, replete with the Easter Beagle. Then he took me to dinner. I was bowled over by his unpretentiousness and kindness.

I would make a dozen week-long visits to Schulz's studio, spending all day long each time with him, from breakfast at the Redwood Arena, an ice rink he'd built for his adopted hometown, until after dinner. We often ate out, usually with his wife Jeannie or one of his five children. I furiously took notes about everything he remembered to tell me. He was a good subject in some ways; his memory was so sharp he could recount entire scenes from childhood. He was a difficult subject, too; his Midwestern reserve left me feeling at the end of some days that he could write a book about me, but I didn't have nearly enough material to flesh out a book about him.

Thinking back, some of the best jewels from Schulz didn't even make the book, which I wrote on a publisher's deadline in less than a year while still churning out four columns a week. One day, while he was drawing and reminiscing aloud, he looked straight at me across his desk and said, "Do you ever wonder why the pages of the Bible are so thin?"

I sensed that he often tried out such left-field lines on friends to watch their reaction and thereby to judge if they'd be good thoughts to use in the strip. I watched for that line in later strips but never saw it. Schulz, by the way, who had the reputation of being a straight arrow, which he was, and religious, which he once had been, characterized himself as a "secular humanist." And so that's what my book said.

Another day, while talking about playing golf with the astronaut Alan Shepard, Schulz let show the petty part of his highly competitive nature. "That drive he hit on the moon was the only good shot he ever made," Schulz said, only partly joking.

When Schulz read my book *Good Grief* before publication, that wonderful quote was one of only two changes he made. He deleted it. It was, after all, an *authorized* biography, and he had veto power over every word. He didn't want to hurt his astronaut friend's feelings. The things he let stay say more about him. He had, for the first time for public consumption, I think, talked openly about his melancholy. That would have been easy to strike from the manuscript, but he did not. Reviewers seized on this aspect of the book after its publication, causing him dismay, but I wrote exactly what he had told me. And he was given the opportunity to excise anything that was wrong or misleading. Truth is, the "good grief" that was alluded to in the double entendre title was not wrong or misleading. Schulz did battle depression as well as mild agoraphobia. I didn't even know what that meant until he explained it to me. This "fear of the marketplace," as the broad definition goes, caused Schulz to prefer to stick to routine and home even though he had ample opportunity to travel. He owned two jets, for heaven's sake.

Schulz was an amalgam of all his cartoon creations. He was philosophical like Linus. Musical like Schroeder. He could be petty and crabby like Lucy. And, obviously, whimsical and creative like Snoopy. Most of all he was Charlie Brown, the kid who didn't get valentines, the man who couldn't quite be happy. Once when we went out to dinner with several of his friends, the waitress brought everyone's meal but Sparky's. It was one of many such Charlie Brown moments.

Schulz and I got along really well, partly because he admired fiction by Southern females, a subject I could explore endlessly without much effort. He especially loved Eudora Welty, and I asked her by letter to write the foreword for the Schulz book. She politely declined, saying she saved every word at that point in her life for her own books. Schulz understood.

Jimmy helped me tremendously with the book, having admired and studied the genius of Schulz most all of his life. Jimmy fed me interesting questions about cartooning to ask on my Santa Rosa visits, and he was uniquely qualified to read and edit my rough draft. Though we'd gone our separate ways, Jimmy was still beside me professionally. I would thank him in the book's acknowledgments, a deserved and minor nod that made life hell for me at home. Barry simply could not handle what was now my strictly platonic relationship with Jimmy.

I began to feel more and more trapped. Some nights when I wasn't up to the inevitable emotional wrestling, I parked my Ford van deep in the woods that headed to the spring. I literally was hiding in my own home. It seems odd now to think that I, this thick-skinned columnist who routinely took on governors and sundry blowhards, could have been that weak. I wasn't being stalked; on his good days I craved this man's attention. Alcoholics all have a charming side. They have to. They must massage you with blue eyes and bouquets to make up for the bullying and intimidation of the night before.

My indecision and infatuation only added to the confusion. I stayed with it a long time, too long, in the name of cutting my losses, I guess. The headlong, impetuous, selfish move I had made in the name of romance had turned and bitten me. The more my professional life soared, the lower my personal life sank.

By now Scripps Howard News Service was distributing the column far and wide to all its subscribers. I often thought how amused my column subjects would have been—especially my political enemies—if they could have seen where my words originated, or seen me for that matter. For a time I wrote on an old red and white enamel kitchen table that had belonged to Jimmy's mother. In the small kitchen with its old-fashioned gas space heater and faux wood paneling, I churned out blistering attacks on politicians and television preachers. I rolled out of my old iron bed in the farmhouse's only bedroom, sometimes wearing my nightgown till noon, typing away in the privacy of my hollow. Every now and again, for lack of a solid idea, I could be downright mean about people who probably didn't deserve my ire. Any columnist who writes for a while occasionally wounds the sparrow instead of the buzzard.

One winter afternoon the wall telephone rang. I was up to my elbows in soap suds, washing last night's dishes. I grabbed the phone with one wet hand.

"Is this Rheta Grimsley Johnson?" a strange little voice asked.

"Yes."

"This is Sonny Bono. Why don't you like me?"

At first I thought the call was a joke, but the distinctive reedy voice sounded just like him. He repeated the question:

"Why don't you like me?"

On a recent slow day, on some feminist rant that I now forget the main point of, I had written a throwaway column about strong women and their weak partners, using the examples of Ike and Tina Turner and Cher and Sonny Bono. I'd made Tina and Cher the heroes, Ike and Sonny the buffoons. Sonny probably hadn't really deserved to be lumped in with the wife-beater Ike, but that kind of thing occasionally happens when a half-baked idea gets served up in print.

Once I'd done explaining to Sonny Bono that I didn't dislike him, at least not personally, I was done with the dishes and ready to tackle another chore. Sonny seemed satisfied to have had his say.

Letters would find their way to the hollow from all sorts of celebrities, including a delightful one from magazine mogul Malcolm Forbes, whose lavish, ballyhooed sixtieth birthday party for Elizabeth Taylor would have been a lot cheaper if held in Iuka, Mississippi, I'd suggested in print. Forbes found the idea funny and said so. He even had been by Iuka, he allowed, while motorcycling on the Natchez Trace.

Mostly, though, the people I interviewed and wrote about were ordinary folks, not celebrities. I had this idea that maybe regular Joes deserved to be in the newspaper more than the usual triumvirate of occasions—at birth, marriage, and death. I wanted to catch them in between those moments, to tell their stories when nobody else bothered. I was mightily influenced by the "home country" period of the late Ernie Pyle, and by Charles Kuralt. With Pyle, it was his disposition I most admired. He had true humility, a kinship with the underdog and a total lack of piety. And though he's known best for his war correspondent days, I loved his American odysseys the best. Kuralt, of course, was a poet, and his short radio essays especially were, in my opinion, the gold standard of human interest writing. They were perfect examples of what I wanted to do, both in terms of subject and evocative short writing. I studied his words the way young artists still wet behind the beret look at a Rembrandt.

It was interesting for me to learn, years after his death, that Kuralt, too, had a rather miserable personal life—if you can assume that keeping two families secret from one another would make a body miserable. I feel safe assuming. He became a media superstar while juggling familial balls in the air. I wonder where he spent most Christmases? Probably on the road, with Charles Kuralt.

In an admittedly half-hearted attempt to end the tempestuous relationship with Barry, I decided to move, to rent a place on the Mississippi Gulf Coast, which had been my favorite seacoast since the Smurf House and Jackson days. I was tired to the bone, too, from the constant home improvement projects at the old farmhouse, especially since few of them measured up to expectations. Usually one team of "carpenters" was followed by another to correct mistakes the first group had made. I was working that old house to death, adding arbors and decks and porches, till the tail wagged the dog in a merciless way. I needed an ocean fix, perhaps an ocean solution.

At first I rented a small house in Gulfport for a couple of months. I liked living there by the ocean so much that it wasn't long before I was looking around for something to buy. The old houses just blocks off the beach were affordable and painted gay, pastel colors, like so many Easter eggs. Hunting a house became my own merry egg hunt and the perfect distraction. I soon found a lovely old sky blue house in nearby Pass Christian, just to the west of Gulfport and Biloxi. It had been built a hundred years earlier and thus had withstood a number of hurricanes, including the monster named Camille.

The blue house was on Second Street, one block from Scenic Drive, which, of course, was oceanfront. The neighborhood was a mix of old and new home sites, landscaped and not. Right across from me was the most interesting old house in town. It appeared ageless and sturdy and falling-in, all at the same time. You never saw or heard a soul there during the day, but sometimes, late at night, a single light would appear in the window and Hank Williams music would float through an open window. I'd sit on my front porch to listen. If I live to be a thousand, I'll always associate that lovely street and house with Hank, his plaintive, soulful poetry bathing me in the sultry nights. It did for me on the edge of the Gulf of Mexico what the lightning bugs had done in the hollow. Hank told me I was home.

Christmas on the coast that year was one of the most beautiful I'd ever experienced. I stood with many others and watched a parade of lighted sailboats float by on the Mississippi Sound. Biloxi even wrapped its famous lighthouse with garland, and I, always appreciating anything nautical, was completely charmed. This seemed about as far away from my troubles as I could run—and still be in Mississippi. I'd always considered its Coast one of the best kept secrets in the world, that is till Katrina roared through a few years later and everyone saw it at its worst.

In the Pass I found temporary peace, and an amazingly diverse community where all the people actually seemed to get along. There were Vietnamese shrimpers, and swells wearing linen togs, million-aires who had migrated from New Orleans to the cooler climate and antebellum mansions with an ocean view. The racial mix was almost equal parts black and white, though at that time, the early 1990s, Pass Christian was majority black and had a black mayor. Many artists and writers and photographers eddied up to the shore, and in the mornings at a cozy restaurant next to the hardware store you could share conversation over grits with the working class, the idle class, or those who refused to be classed.

Scripps Howard sent me to Barcelona and the Olympics in 1992, the year I was reveling in discovering the Mississippi Coast in-depth. Spain was an exciting assignment, and a world away from my troubles. I was grateful that I kept getting paid to travel and learn. I often couldn't believe my good luck, working for newspapers outside of the newsrooms, missing all the meetings and bureaucracy that had finally found my trade, pretty much setting my own schedule and pace. That is, as long as I turned in the requisite columns, no small chore.

In Spain one day I took a train ride from Barcelona to an outlying community which had a small museum that included in its myriad of exhibits a stuffed black man under glass. In the name of science, some Victorian explorer had exhumed the anonymous body and it ended up as a museum curiosity. The town had been chosen as the Olympic rowing venue and a few athletes and some sponsors took exception to plying the waters in a town that would display a stuffed human being. But eventually rowing came to town, and the body stayed.

That's the kind of column I looked for when covering political conventions or the Olympics. There were enough sports reporters to handle the sports, enough political reporters to handle the politics. I sought out the stories that fell through the cracks when assignments were made. I'd always liked the oddball idea and avoided the press conference. Somehow, in a business run by opinionated editors, I got away with it.

I hadn't been home from Spain or back in the blue house near the ocean for long when the telephone rang one night. The voice sounded like Ben Johnson, the actor who played Sam the Lion in *The Last Picture Show*. This was a slow, melodious, Mississippi Gulf Coast voice, nothing shrill or businesslike about it. I had heard it before, though I couldn't put a name with it. Something about the cadence was distinctive and soothing.

Don Grierson, a journalism professor at the University of Alabama Birmingham—UAB—was calling to offer me a one-shot, ten-week job teaching advanced feature writing. The pay was great, the hours something I could handle on top of the column, and that voice, well, it seemed to hold all the sorrow and wisdom and serenity abroad in the world. I had met Don briefly when he taught at Mississippi State. I'd spoken to one of his journalism classes there one day. I couldn't remember for certain how to pronounce his last name—on the Coast in Moss Point where he's from it's GRI-son, rhymes with bison—or much about him, honestly. But I remembered that calming voice. After hesitating for about ten seconds, I said "Yes."

My new duties would begin right after Christmas break, Don said, which he planned to spend squirrel hunting.

# 14

# The Poppy Field

The old farm in the hollow pretty much took care of itself in the wintertime. The grass didn't grow and the house didn't mildew and the termites took a rest. Unless there was an ice storm, the trees just kept on growing. I ran enough gas heat to keep the pipes from bursting, and I'd go home often enough to keep the burglars guessing. The place had been so cheap to buy that I'd paid the bank off quickly, and property taxes in Mississippi are next to nothing. I saw no reason to sell it.

It looked sad and neglected when I'd drive up from the coast. I sometimes thought of it as a child I had abandoned to go off and live a more carefree life. That couldn't be helped, I figured. I'd renewed my tenuous relationship with Barry, but now it had geographical limits that kept it saner. The length of a state can do a lot for some romances. I felt an obligation but not much of anything else. He'd had a small stroke and almost simultaneously lost his health and his health insurance, dropped when he quit a county job on principle. He was, despite his faults, an honest and principled man.

In the springtime I spent more time in the hollow. For one thing, I was commuting each Monday morning to Birmingham and my feature-writing class. The students were bright and eager; they had been hand-picked by Don for their acumen. I looked forward to the sessions, but, more than the class, to seeing Don once a week. He had the most beatific countenance, the most stable demeanor of anyone I'd ever known. I craved his quiet, steady ways and his kindness. He loved Hank Williams music and Matthew Arnold poetry and *The Beverly Hillbillies* on TV. He lived alone and frugally in an old single-wide house trailer at the foot of a hill at the lakeside home of his older brother, Buba, and Buba's true love, Annie. Don took me there to meet them, and I fell completely, happily in love with Smith Lake and the contented life they all seemed to live. I even began to appreciate the trailer, which, in a touch of irony, had in rubber script on its front the name "PARK AVENUE."

And I fell hopelessly in love with Don.

I told Barry. I didn't name names, but I did say I'd found someone else I wanted to see and thought we should end our long and tortured friendship. My confession released torrents of anger and recrimination. But, as the days passed, and finally a couple of weeks, I found hope that Barry had accepted the situation. He said that he had.

We could be friends, we decided. Barry even helped me sow the pasture beside my house with poppy seeds. I had mixed them with damp sand like the instructions suggested, and I sat on the tailgate of his truck and broadcast fists full of seeded sand while Barry slowly made circles in the grass. It was a good day. Our last.

That last week of his life Barry kept all his legal appointments, endured a root canal, and ate and drank with friends. He came by the farmhouse a couple of times, including the day I was packing to spend the weekend in Pass Christian. He asked to come along, make a holiday of it, but I said "No," and that I had other plans. Turns out he didn't need my permission. After stopping several times to see friends on the seven-hour trip to Pass Christian, Barry pulled up into my oyster-shell driveway about two hours after I had arrived. I went out and asked him to leave. He was furious, shouting threats, making drunken demands.

Barry did not die instantly, even though he pointed the gun straight at his own fair temple and fired it straight into his brain. It would take hours for him to die. I would watch and weep as the excess blood from his bandaged head poured into a stainless steel box fitted beneath the hospital bed. His hands were wrapped in brown paper bags to preserve the gunpowder that proved his death was a suicide. His blue eyes were wide open. His stubborn heart outlasted his brain. When finally it was over, the sun was beginning to rise over the seacoast that in the past, in the lovely Pass, had brought me comfort and joy. The rosy color of predawn seemed like a bloody nightmare to me now.

I was told by someone, I can't remember who, that I was not welcome at his funeral. But I made the long drive home to the hollow that day anyway. It just seemed like the thing to do. I sat on my own front porch and waited. I didn't know what I was waiting for. A few of his friends came by after the service. His sister, a wonderful woman who perhaps knew her brother better than anyone else, came and stayed, holding me and telling me again and again not to blame myself.

I did, of course. Even though Barry's closest friends had heard him threaten suicide more than once, none of us really believed he would make good on the threats. He had a broad manipulative streak, and we all figured such a threat was part and parcel of getting his way. He fooled us. He made good on the threat all right, and on my watch.

I wasn't the only one who needed to blame me for Barry's death. Those in town who had been at the receiving end of his generosity—and they were legion—had to blame somebody. Many had never seen the dark side of the Barry moon. I was the logical one to blame. The usual small-town rumors flew: He'd been at the Coast casinos and had lost a fortune at the blackjack table. He'd been shot by my lover. He had aimed at me and missed and hit himself. And, of course, he hadn't committed suicide at all. I had shot him.

Barry died in May. By Christmas I had rented out the blue house by the ocean to a couple of newlyweds. For me the place was too sad to see, much less inhabit. I had moved myself back to the hollow where I lived like a hermit, writing the column and making only quick trips to the grocery when necessary. It might have made more sense to live on the coast, which I had so enjoyed, and to sell the farmhouse where I suddenly had few friends and only bad memories. But I couldn't even drive up the driveway to the blue house without breaking down. One house was the devil, the other the deep blue sea.

In Iuka I felt like a pariah at worst, a curiosity at best. I was like the stuffed man in the little Spanish museum, a macabre curiosity that people pointed at and turned quickly away from. I could count on one hand the people who offered condolences. And the looks in the Piggly-Wiggly aisles were enough to curdle my half gallon of milk.

I kept working, but, for once in my life, I don't remember a single column from the year following Barry's death. I already had taken my vacation, and the Memphis editor was sympathetic but wouldn't agree to the month of unpaid leave that I asked for. So, out of habit and by rote, I kept writing the column. I'd become a member of a secret society made up of people who have lost a loved one to suicide. I can see it in a face now and know. Or at least I think I can.

Of all those poppy seeds we spread that last day, only one flower bloomed. I was surprised when I saw it; I had forgotten about the seeds, the day, the satisfying feeling of watching for something to wrestle its way out of the ground. There are a thousand ways to die. It's much, much harder to live.

That Christmas was the saddest of my life, something to be gotten through instead of enjoyed. There were no lighted sailboats, no lightning bugs, no Smurf figurines dangling from a lopsided cedar. I don't really remember much about it, which is probably a good thing. Annie, Buba, and Don all tried to help, to cheer me, but some journeys are solitary and must be traveled.

I do remember thinking about Pop's cedar branch and its colored lights. Maybe he wasn't just a frugal farmer with no inclination to decorate lavishly for the holidays. I suddenly wondered if life had pruned his decorations down to that minimalist look we as children had thought so wonderful. Maybe it was all the cheer he could muster.

# 15

# Grizzard Is Dead
# and I Don't Feel So Good Myself

N ext to Texas, Georgia probably is mentioned in more songs than any other state. An old newspaper buddy of mine, John Branston, makes the case for Texas, and, being a Georgia native, I cheer for the home team.

"'Waltz Across Texas,'" John will say out of nowhere when I see him.

"'Midnight Train to Georgia,'" I counter.

"'Yellow Rose of Texas,' not Georgia," John says.

"Georgia's on our minds, not Texas."

We've been at it for years. Even if she doesn't win the prize, I think Georgia deserves it. And, yes, I think of Georgia as female. There's something both mystical and musical about the place, with its watermelon-colored clay and its unifying comforter of kudzu. If there's a sweeter smell than the purple kudzu bloom in the summertime I don't know it. The air suddenly is full of grape popsicles, and you don't want to stand still too long for fear of wearing a kudzu coat.

As a child I had a friend named Georgia, and I envied her the name.

Why couldn't I have been named Georgia Grimsley, especially since girls with alliterative names were always prettier and more popular? Cathy Caddell, Mary Maples. Jennifer Jones. And Georgia Grimsley.

The iconic Southern humorist Lewis Grizzard died in May 1994, leaving a gaping hole in that prestigious bit of journalistic real estate called the *Atlanta Journal Constitution*. I'd been happy for fourteen years with the *Commercial Appeal*, the only union paper in the South and thus one of the best-paying. But I'll have to say, the Atlanta paper was where you were supposed to *want* to go if you were a reporter in the South. It had the prestige, the reputation, and a contrail of writers who had left and gone on to write best-selling novels and screenplays and such. Plus it had columnist Celestine Sibley, a rare female legend in the business. She had been writing her human interest column for more than five decades in Atlanta. I had met her once, when she gave a speech in Huntsville. But I imagined having lunch with her, becoming good friends, comparing notes on how hard it is to climb the glass hill of deadlines for decades. She'd been at it a lot longer than I and must know some secrets, I reasoned.

I'd almost gone to the *AJC* in 1988 when hotshot editor Bill Kovach offered me a columnist job. I'd won a spate of prizes about that time, and both Atlanta and the *Philadelphia Inquirer*—with its three top editors from the South—made interesting offers. An editor from the *Inquirer* newsroom, Jim Naughton, even drove an old baby blue Mustang down from Pennsylvania and left it parked in my front yard in the hollow with a note that said for me to drive it back up to Philadelphia when I joined his staff. I had turned down both good offers and stayed put in Mississippi and with the *Commercial Appeal*. I felt some sort of obligation to dance with the one who brung me, as the saying goes.

Atlanta, by the time Grizzard died, had a new editor in Ron Martin. And I, for the first time, had plenty of good reasons to leave Mississippi. When Ron phoned out of the blue one night and offered me the column slot left vacant by Grizzard, I said "Yes." It seemed like fate had lent a hand. I was just to continue doing what I'd been doing for many years, he explained, only now my home newspaper would be the *Atlanta* by-god *Constitution*.

I was pumped, both with relief and enthusiasm. A new start in my home state. Might be just what the doctor ordered. I borrowed a bed and a mattress and a truck to haul them in from Buba and Annie. I headed east on a Sunday, determined to make a name for myself in Georgia, even if my name wasn't Georgia. In my first column for the storied newspaper, I introduced myself by writing with sincere affection about childhood summers spent in Georgia.

*. . . To ride with my grandfather was to run with the bulls in Pamplona, to tip a glass heavenward. He had a parcel of land he called Egypt. We would climb into the dusty International, point it toward Egypt and sing like banshees. "In the sweet . . . gimme some meat . . . by and by . . . gimme some pie. When we meet on that beautiful shore . . . gimme me some more.*

*We swam in a creek called Williams' Mill. Old Man Williams had hauled in white sand to make a beach. The cows didn't respect the beach, otherwise it was perfect.*

*All my relatives read the* Constitution. *A lot of them cussed it. My grandfather would sit on the front porch, his brogans crossed like swords and propped high on the porch railing, reading the good stories aloud.*

*"Listen to this," he'd say. "Dateline: Columbus." He always said the "dateline" part, like an old-fashioned radio announcer.*

*Today I drove into Atlanta for my first day at work for the* Journal-

Constitution. *From a hazy distance, the city looked like an overwrought dream.*

*I saw The Varsity, still hopping. I saw the newspaper, the one where Ralph McGill worked, the one where Celestine Sibley works.*

*My grandfather, had he lived too long, would have been 100 this summer. He would have been amazed to see my name in his paper.*

*I want to write stories he might have read aloud. Or the kind my grandmother might have clipped and folded and tucked between Proverbs and Ecclesiastes . . .*

You get the drift. I was perfectly aware I was treading hallowed ground, but I felt reverence for different reasons than many thought I should. I'll never forget seeing my rodeo-star cousin Marshall soon after I took the job. "You're trying to fill some mighty big shoes," he said, meaning Grizzard's. He gave me a withering, disapproving look, and that was all.

I would not be billed as Grizzard's replacement; the editors had that much sense. But I arrived a month after his death, and my column ran where his long had. A lot of his readers and fans were rabidly unhappy with the decision to replace Lewis with a woman. Especially a liberal woman, one who went to Auburn instead of Georgia, and one whose essays usually included more angst than humor.

My second column for the *AJC*—after the love note to Georgia—was about a gay country music singer from Tupelo. That was all it took. Letters arrived by the bushel, angry letters, most of them telling me to go back to Mississippi, do not collect $200. I wasn't worthy of carrying Grizzard's typewriter. There were even attacks, in print in my own newspaper, from new colleagues, including the venerable sports columnist Furman Bisher. As college newspaper editor at Auburn I had carefully budgeted the $200 to pay Bisher to come and speak at our year-end banquet. Now he was the enemy.

The Radio Right went ballistic. Atlanta talk radio is as virulent as it gets, and on any given day I could hear the right-wing kooks blasting me and my column by name. They kept it up for seven years.

Looking back, I think many readers simply felt it might have been best not to hire another columnist at all after Grizzard died. Just leave the space blank. And many long, lonely days my first year in Atlanta I would have agreed with them.

With the Scripps Howard newspaper company I'd always been given the freedom to write about whatever I wanted. About a third of my column repertoire was political. In Atlanta, after I got there, it was strongly suggested that I veer away from politics and stick to human interest subjects. They had a whole floor of political columnists, the editor said. I was to write four columns a week, and for the first year, at least, they should all be datelined Georgia. So much for doing what I'd been doing.

I was forty. An old dog, especially in columnist years. I'd been extremely lucky, having things my way for a long, long time. Suddenly I had conflicting column suggestions bombarding me from half a dozen editors. The Atlanta newsroom was chief-heavy. For years I'd been free to roam the South, hell, the nation, and now I was told to stop at the Georgia state line.

It wasn't just the job description that was troubling. I had to get used to the city. There were more people working in the *AJC* office building than lived in my adopted hometown of Iuka. Traffic was hellish, living up to its national reputation. And in the midst of the fiery job baptism, I had to find a place to live. I first rented a trailer in the western suburb of Douglasville, simply because it was close to the Alabama line, which was as close as I could get to Mississippi and still be technically in Georgia.

Only one thing turned out as I had dreamed it might be. Though neither of us ever found the time to become close friends, Celestine Sibley was as wonderful as I had suspected. My first full day at work, she came down to my desk and invited me to lunch. I marveled at how much copy the octogenarian turned out. I couldn't complain about my workload, four columns a week, because she was doing the same number of columns plus writing books on the side. I decided she must not drink at all, else she'd never have had the energy. Then she asked me to lunch again. This time we were invited to a fancy downtown club with former *Constitution* editor Hal Gulliver. I was thrilled to go along.

The two old newspaper pals ordered Bloody Mary's before lunch, then a bottle of white wine with lunch. Every time I emptied a glass, Gulliver filled it. I was feeling no pain by the time we had dessert. I said my goodbyes, leaving a pair of prescription eyeglasses somewhere between the club and the car. I had to go straight home and sleep it off. Celestine, on the other hand, who had at least as much as I did to drink, went back to the office and pounded out a perfect column. She was the consummate professional.

I was so homesick and tired that first year that I thought more than once about leaving, admitting my failure, and tucking tail. But I didn't. I'd arrived in June and decided to see if I could make it to Christmas. Maybe by Christmas things would get better. Maybe by Christmas my kind of readers would find me. Maybe by Christmas I'd be out of the Douglasville trailer and living in a nice house befitting the best-paying job I'd ever had in journalism. Maybe by Christmas the world would come to an end and none of this petty stuff would matter anyhow.

Christmas came. It always does.

She was a pretty picture, a smiling Macy's gift wrap clerk, wearing bouncing gold earrings and a red lamb's wool sweater. The coat to be wrapped for Don was hanging on a nice wooden hanger, and the comely clerk hesitated before tossing the hanger into the garbage. "Do you want to keep this?"

"No," I said. "I have too far to walk."

"If you're walking, it would make a pretty good weapon," she said, waving the hanger in a swashbuckling demonstration.

I thought about the scene walking back through the downtown Macy's, a walk of only a few blocks from the *AJC* building. I rarely found time to shop during the day, but it was getting really close to Christmas and I'd decided on a camel's hair coat for Don. A choir was singing about good will toward men. The whole fancy department store was a fantasy, a foil-wrapped world that smelled like gingerbread and expensive perfumes. But, outside, you needed a weapon.

I was feeling a little sorry for myself, granted. Like the rube that I was, I'd left valuables in a locked car, in plain sight, in a downtown parking lot. The safety glass was in a green pile on the red back seat. The crime was in the colors of the season. I didn't even notice the loss until traffic eased at the edge of town, I picked up speed and the cold air hit. A mild big-city initiation, as they go. But I no longer felt the way I'd felt the Sunday I'd driven to Georgia from Mississippi. That day I'd given a big honk on the Ford's horn as I crossed the state line, exuberant about the possibilities.

"I'm coming home!" I said aloud to myself.

It wouldn't take too long to realize I'd done no such thing. I wasn't coming home. I had left it.

# 16

# Finding Neverland

Don was a fixture in my life now. He had been patient while I mourned for a man whose violence will forever haunt me. He had not rushed me or even phoned till I was ready for contact. Don had moved in that slow, mysterious way of his to become an indispensable, reassuring presence. I could no longer imagine living without him or why I would want to.

We thought alike, about everything from artichokes to zoos, abortion to Zola. We didn't agree on guns—he was a collector—or on Christmas—he found it depressing. I liked to dance but he balked at that, declaring "All dancers are exhibitionists." But other than those things we were spookily compatible. We soon bought a house in Carrollton, Georgia, once again locating as close to Mississippi as the State of Alabama would allow. Don was still teaching journalism at UAB, but he commuted to Carrollton on weekends and sometimes came home after his night classes during the week. It was tough, but he was, too.

His life had not been easy. You might say in his family he'd been the fall crop. He was ten years younger than Buba, eleven years younger than the oldest sibling, Jim. It had fallen to Don to take care of his elderly father after his mother died at age sixty-eight. Don would drive from his teaching post in Starkville to the Mississippi coast nearly every weekend for eight years to visit his father, and, eventually, to check him out of the nursing home for weekend diversions.

Don had been married and divorced once, same as I, and remained close friends with his English teacher ex. She was an accomplished poet and shared Don's love of literature. So he understood my feelings for Jimmy and respected them. Don was not the complaining type. Not about anything. I never heard him describe an ailment aloud, or say how tired he was, though when he was tired it showed in his eyes. He didn't talk a lot, period. But, when he did, my journalism experience made me want to take notes. When Don talked, he had something to say. He believed in what he always described as "narrative economy." He said everyone, regardless of profession, should take one journalism course in life to learn to edit their oral stories.

He was a small man, or maybe I'm just a large woman. We were exactly the same height, five-eight, and wore the same shoe size. He did not have that Napoleonic complex you hear so much about. Anything but. He was as comfortable in his own skin as anyone I've ever known, male or female. He knew his strengths and played to them. He was cerebral but not academic. He was sexy but not particularly romantic. He was liberal but not of the limousine variety. He loved to read but mostly stuck with the classics. He was worldly but not pretentious. He drank Jack Daniels almost every day I knew him, but I only saw him drunk once. From September till spring you wouldn't have picked him out of a crowd of camouflage-wearing rednecks, except he could quote Shakespeare and Sartre and often sat around reading both.

He was, in a word, perfect. Don didn't have the glamorous looks of Barry, a poor woman's Paul Newman, or the patience of Jimmy, who gave Job a run for his money. But Don loved me, I knew it, and we were both old enough and mature enough to appreciate the odds against this ever happening again for either of us. We embraced it, and each other.

The Carrollton house sat right next to the Little Tallapoosa River. We could drop a canoe into the river from our backyard and float ten miles without seeing another soul. The location was unusual, to say the least, so close to Atlanta, and a farmer's four hundred acres surrounding us gave the illusion of being in the woods. The bucolic setting beckoned after days in Atlanta's traffic, and we grew to love the old house and its history. We had bought it from a personable electrician named Rudy, the nephew of the man who once had owned the grist mill that still stood at the site.

Rudy's predilection for all things electrical showed up in the outlets lined up four abreast on every wall, not to mention in tree trunks outside, and in random speakers and sprinkler systems and all manner of security lights. We were definitely plugged in.

The Rudy estate even had a homemade swimming pool, which Don compared to keeping a baby in the backyard. "It always needs something," he said.

Chelsey and Ben were just the right age to enjoy a swimming pool, so the timing was perfect. Chelsey spent one entire visit in pink rubber fins, refusing to take them off even to eat or nap. Ben loved the canoe trips down the Little Tallapoosa. And I transformed the old millhouse into a little theater for Chelsey, whose dramatic flair had grown along with her. I even bought an orange and blue neon sign that lit up the riverbank and said, of course, "Chelsey's Playhouse."

Atlanta won the competition to host the 1996 Olympics, which didn't mean much to me. The *AJC* had its own Olympic coverage team, which I was not a part of despite my experience covering the games in both Los Angeles and Barcelona. I didn't much care. The main benefit I saw came in a directive from the newspaper hierarchy to staff: Stay at home and work if you can. We should do our part to ease the traffic during the Olympics.

I was delighted. It really made little sense for me to fight the traffic getting to the newsroom each day just to have to fight my way out again a few minutes later to begin the column hunt. I loved working from home, or from the road, and the Olympics directive threw me into that briar patch of solitary work once again. After the Olympics ended and almost everyone else went back to their newsroom desks, I kept working from home most days. Nobody seemed to notice or care. I had hit my stride, searching the back roads for stories that the metro reporters weren't interested in pursuing. Under the heading of "houses" alone I scored scoops: I found a former Jimmy Carter aide who lived in a tree house made from an old airplane, a monk turned atheist who built a hexagonal house, an eccentric who stretched his dream home over a river using an old steel bridge for the foundation.

I interviewed a few celebrities, including the actress Dixie Carter who offered something original: "It takes a good man to be better than no man at all," she said when I told her I admired her husband, the actor Hal Holbrook.

Mostly, though, I stuck to my creed about featuring mostly ordinary people in my column. God knows there were enough *AJC* writers covering celebrities. I went out to eat with two other newspaper reporters one night—one of them a sportswriter, the other the movie reviewer—and through idle conversation found I was the only one of us three who didn't know Paul Newman personally. When Princess Di died, the paper sent a columnist to London to cover her funeral. They sent me to Luthersville, Georgia, to cover the funeral of a poor black man buried the same day, if not in the same way. I much preferred my assignment.

At the end of the long work day, there was Don. We often sat on a deck we built ourselves, mostly singing and strumming guitars. Don could do a dead-on Hank impression, and he'd sing "Cold, Cold Heart" and "Be Careful of Stones That You Throw." There were few hours of relief for me between the time I finished one column and the worry of what I'd write about next. The hot whips of panic were on my back continually.

Looking back, I marvel that I lasted seven years in Atlanta. I would not have, but for Don. Sharing life with him made everything bearable. He knew what was important, what was not. No amount of money is worth ruining your health, he'd say again and again, and I knew he was right.

Don marveled that I still got excited about Christmas. He could not. Too many sad memories decked his halls, he said. So the second year of my *AJC* job, we booked a trip to England for what the British descriptively call "the run-up to Christmas." We stayed in the sheep-trading town of Chipping Camden in the Cotswolds.

When the plane landed at Gatwick, snow was on the ground and on the roses still in bloom. The weather was lovely for the whole trip, and our historic hotel was one that King George II had used on a visit. Night came early in December, and the shop windows full of Christmas goodies literally twinkled in the early twilight. We walked the hills each day, sharing the paths with sheep and other livestock and plenty of fellow hikers. We marveled at the serenity and cleanliness of the English countryside.

Don's love and knowledge of English literature made the trip richer than it might have been. We took the train to Oxford one day, and to Dover another. Don's favorite poem was "Dover Beach," and we stood on the white cliffs and saw for ourselves where ignorant armies, time after time, had clashed at night. We saw relics from the Sutton Ho in London's fabulous British Museum, and we spent an hour by ourselves next to Shakespeare's tomb at the church in Stratford. In the cozy pubs we enjoyed the peat fires and warm company, not to mention the inexpensive and delicious "pub grub."

For some reason, our seat assignments for the return trip to Atlanta were not together. I sat next to a charming ten-year-old from London whose father now lived in Charleston, South Carolina. The girl was addressing Christmas cards and reading a child's abridged version of *King Lear*. Don was somewhere in front of me, reading his book and making awkward small talk with a stranger. At some point during the long flight he turned, grinned, and waved. I remember thinking then of Dixie Carter's wonderful quote: it takes a very good man to be better than no man at all.

# 17

# Poor Man's Provence

Chelsey said the best advice I ever gave her was this: "Always have a trip planned. You'll then have something to look forward to, a big crisp carrot to trot behind on drab or downright bad days, powerful incentive to finish any task at hand."

"That *is* pretty wise advice," I replied, not remembering it at all. "I said that?"

"Well, you said, 'Always have a trip planned.'"

Chelsey inherited my need to embellish, to make people sound better than they actually are, to wear rose-colored glasses when it comes to humanity.

She needed money for a school trip to Spain.

For once, I was taking my own advice. Don and I almost always had a trip planned during our first decade together—to Ireland, France, Key West, San Francisco, Alaska, and Charleston. Many of our domestic trips combined business and pleasure, which meant the Atlanta newspaper paid for them. The *AJC* spared no expense sending its people far and wide for a good story, or even a mediocre one. Most of our travel, in fact, was at the paper's behest. The best thing was the

*AJC* never once looked askance at an expense report. Not so long as you came back with a story.

At smaller papers, I'd gotten used to traveling on the cheap, staying at the Red Roof Inn, not the Ritz-Carlton. Usually you could work just about any story you wanted, but only if you made it affordable for the editorial budget. I became an expert at "living out loud," as former *New York Times* columnist Anna Quindlen aptly called it, mining for journalistic meaning during trips I didn't much mind taking anyway. I slept on the floor of an Associated Press reporter friend's Manhattan walk-up to write stories from the Big Apple, and showered at the KOA Campground to get to venture out West. Once my favorite Memphis editor, Michael Grehl, posted my expense report on the bulletin board after I stayed an entire week in New Orleans for less than $200, counting meals, during the World's Fair there; he wanted other reporters to follow my frugal example. That expense report didn't make me popular with anyone but the editor. I sure ate a lot of Lucky Dogs.

I was always honest about expenses, carefully excluding Don's half of every meal we took, paying for thank-you gifts for column subjects out of my own pocket. But I had a little fun with it, too. Once, on one of my expense reports, I added a few dollars and listed the cost of a case of .22 cartridges for my buddy Whiskey Gray after he took his entire day ferrying me around Tennessee to potential column spots. The ammo was a thank you I figured the newspaper owed. The paper paid.

In Atlanta there was no need to squeeze every expense dime. That newspaper, like a society maven who wears all her gold to the country club, wanted its reporters to look respectable. That management attitude often was abused. One Atlanta sports reporter I knew would purposely seek out the most expensive hotel in any town where he was sent. "Might as well," he reasoned. "Somebody in features will spend it if we don't."

There were limits, even in Atlanta. The *AJC* was slow to see merit in the French stories I pitched. I was sincere, for instance, in thinking that the Parisian embrace of black Southern gospel music would make good Atlanta copy. Half a dozen Paris radio stations featured the music exclusively in the late 1990s. It was a regular phenomenon, as I saw it. Could I help it if chasing that story involved flying to France? But my reputation as the Francophile made that particular suggestion suspect. The paper wasn't buying it.

Don and I went to France anyway, on our own dime, several times. In 1996 we went to the Dordogne on a long vacation that meant before taking off I wrote sixteen columns in advance. Writing a topical column in advance is akin to grieving before the death.

The day we left I was almost too tired to present a passport. It proved worth the effort, though, when we arrived by rental car at the stone mill house near Bergerac that four of us had booked for an entire month. A little lagoon outlined by stones dominated the front yard, and storybook sheep wandered the hillsides nearby. On the stone cottage itself, built seven hundred years earlier, red roses cascaded. There were dormer windows from which you expected Rapunzel to be dropping her ponytail. It was as if every fantastic, unreasonable childhood dream I'd ever had about my favorite country was unfolding on cue. Upon our arrival, seeing all this, I cried like Meryl Streep, much to the annoyance of my traveling companions who didn't have so much riding on expectations.

France had seemed to me the place to be since high school. At the unlikely Robert E. Lee High in the Heart of Dixie I'd had a young French teacher whose hair was galvanized with Aqua Net into the perfect "flip," and whose short skirts and high heels had a mildly exotic look. She even made radio commercials for the local drugstore's French perfumes. French women, she told us, are more beautiful because they use all their facial muscles when they speak. She would demonstrate with an exaggerated and slow-motion pronunciation that used her high cheeks and big lips to great effect. We would "répétez" with gusto, hoping one day if we conjugated enough French verbs we'd look like her.

Yes, I had a romanticized, twinkling idea of Paris and the rest of it, a 1940s' musical vision with pink poodles, navy berets, and Edith Piaf singing "La Vie en Rose" perpetually in the background. Fact is, France never disappointed. The women *were* beautiful, whether it had to do with enunciating and facial muscles or not. The men were beautiful, too, so help me, as was the countryside.

There was a lot of sitting about the fairy-tale house, reading and eating and congratulating ourselves on having found such a place. We also wore the wheels off the rental car. We explored the cave cities of troglodytes, watched the local sunflower crop mature, ate inexpensive, memorable, four-hour meals at a local ferme auberge, drank amazing wine for pennies a glass, canoed on the Dordogne River, people-watched in the medieval city of Sarlat, and flew home desperately in love with the southwest French countryside.

I never got over it.

It wasn't just the incomparable beauty of the French landscape. My passion had evolved from the romantic notions instilled at Lee High. I couldn't help but noticing I agreed with most French priorities, which seemed to be, in no particular order, beauty, books, food, and flowers, and all their intersections. France also was a country that prized its intellectuals, unlike ours which has only disdain for higher learning in the truest sense. France was a country where everyone went to theater and museums, where you could buy a book from a sidewalk vending machine, a place perfumed by its culture and love of learning. And it provided health care for all its citizens.

I started celebrating Bastille Day each year, confounding both Georgia and Mississippi neighborhoods in their turn with fireworks and flapping red, white, and blue French flags on July 14. It might have seemed silly to others, but at times it kept me sane. It kept me believing in a country, a people, during times when I couldn't quite believe in my own.

Don might not have had quite the enthusiasm I did for devoting a week of our lives to preparations for Bastille Day, but he was a sport. He, too, admired the French. The party grew from a porch table with eight guests, to a side yard with eighty, and by sheer will I made it a hot ticket in our little town. One requirement was that you bring to the party with you a reverence for all things French, much like the "simplicity of heart" that was the ticket to a Jay Gatsby party. When people repeated stupid or stereotypical remarks about the French, they lost their place at future parties. The more I pared the guest list, the more some wanted to attend.

For a time Bastille Day even took the place of Christmas in my heart and on my social calendar. I put as much effort into decorating and baking and cleaning for the French national holiday as I did for an American Christmas. It made some kind of visceral sense to me, being patriotic to a land where I'd never really belong. Turns out, I was practicing.

Though we would return to France half a dozen times in the next few years, we never once made it to Provence. I read all of the Peter Mayle books on the region, laughing out loud at his attempts to fit in while settling in. But, I did not go. It's almost as if that mythical region was meant to remain only in my imagination, its lavender fields and romance too powerful to unleash into real memory, even mine. But soon, and for the oddest work-related reason, that omission ceased to matter.

One fall day in 1996, my supervising editor George Edmondson called me in to talk over a story suggestion. George wasn't dogmatic, but he was conscientious. He'd often pitch stories, ones that he thought suited both me and the Atlanta readers, and I usually tried to agree. Often they were related to country music, a genre we both enjoyed. Because of George I got to cover "Writers' Night" at Nashville's famous Bluebird Café, where an unlikely looking novice songwriter from Ohio sang "I'd Rather Drink This Beer in Hell Alone, Than Drink It Here With You." I attended Hank Snow's funeral at the Ryman and interviewed the legendary Kitty Wells.

Wonderful assignments, all. But this time the story was about wild hogs, not country pickers. George had seen an ad in *Soldier of Fortune* magazine selling a "wild boar hunt" at a southwest Louisiana compound called Boarbusters Hunting Lodge. He thought a hog hunt might make good copy.

It wasn't my favorite idea ever, but I obliged and made arrangements to accompany a group of young Baton Rouge working men on a bow hunt one fall Saturday. Don was off work for the weekend and went along. He loved southwest Louisiana, true Cajun Country, and we both thought there might be a chance to look around once the hunt ended.

It ended quickly; the first arrow that flew pierced not one but two hogs, much to the dismay of the young hunters. They hadn't counted on a double kill and the resulting per-hog fee. Don and I thanked the hunters and the Boarbusters crew, and then quickly found our way to the swamp and the nearest marina.

The place was called Basin Landing, and there on the edge of the Atchafalaya Swamp we found her: a shanty boat that would forever alter our lives. The *Green Queen*, a funky old houseboat with vinyl siding the color of dinner mints, wore two signs that day. There was the one telling us her name—the *Green Queen*—and another that said "For Sale." It was the second sign, of course, that got us in trouble.

Don was the one who usually kept a heavy foot on the brakes of practicality. But this day duck-hunting possibilities overrode his sensible nature. By the time we drove home to Carrollton, we'd convinced ourselves that somehow we had time in our busy lives to enjoy a little houseboat on the Atchafalaya Swamp. Why, we'd stay on our boat during Don's long break between Thanksgiving and January. I could find lots of stories in the area. So long as I kept feeding the monster—filing daily columns to the insatiable newspaper—nobody would care that I was bobbing amongst the water hyacinths in Louisiana instead of beating the metro Atlanta pavement. Well, maybe they'd care a little.

There was no debate about where to spend Christmas after that. The duck season begins each year around Thanksgiving and lasts through January. Christmas would fall smack dab in the middle, and though there is a first and second half of duck season with a break in between, the break never includes Christmas day. Christmas is a minor blip on the radar screen of real hunters. That was okay with me. I had great plans for making the *Green Queen* the cutest floating vessel in the Atchafalaya Swamp, beginning with a big Christmas wreath for the front door. I even found a string of lights with the Budweiser frogs and beer bottles.

By the time we got to the *Green Queen* a few days before Christmas, the nearby town of Henderson had been bedecked with more loving exuberance than I'd ever witnessed. Anything that wouldn't wander off to graze was wrapped in lights. Propane tanks, water meters, tool sheds, cars on cinder blocks. Everything wore Christmas colors. Holiday symbols were mixed with abandon. The Wise Men marched in step with Santa's elves. The Star of Bethlehem shone over Santa's workshop. The crèche at the Catholic church—the center of social and civic activity—was elevated, situated on the bell tower above the head of another Mother Mary. Ice skaters twirled around a "frozen" pond in eighty-degree weather. It was delightful.

Don took off each morning before light, and I fell back asleep before the roar of his outboard faded. He had made friends with other hunters, and usually had a companion in the pre-dawn swamp. I, on the other hand, knew no one. I'm not much at mingling with strangers unless there's column incentive, and I really wanted a brief break from work. So I read a stack of books, wrote postcards telling people what a fine holiday we were having in the Louisiana swamp and ate myself silly at every mealtime. As Christmases go, or the run-up to them, it was a tad lonely. I'd left a fine, decorated tree back in Georgia, and the Green Queen seemed a tad cheerless and empty despite my best efforts. But whenever Don returned, he lit up the boat with his enthusiasm and endless tales from the swamp. He was happier than I'd ever seen him, plucking and cleaning his ducks off the back porch of the little houseboat, describing for me the natural scene that changed on a daily basis. I was envious of the sense of purpose he had in this place, a routine that gave structure to his holiday. I, on the other hand, was freed up from shopping, decorating, and, temporarily, writing, which left me with nervous energy to burn.

One day before Christmas I was in the marina store, buying a

Coke or looking for Don, when a little girl poked her head from around the counter. She was the granddaughter of Jeanette Latiolais, who, along with her husband, Johnelle, ran the marina. It had been Johnelle who sold us the *Green Queen*. Johnelle's a super salesman, but he didn't even have to pull his tools from the bag that day. The *Green Queen* sold itself.

Don already had fallen in love with the gregarious Latiolais couple, but I'd shied from the store, a virtual taxidermy museum of mounted albino squirrels and deer heads. The place teemed with boaters and hunters, most of them cheerfully swapping raucous tales in Cajun French. Whenever I'd venture inside, I was the only soul not wearing camouflage or speaking Cajun. I was what was wrong with this picture every time.

This day was different. The store was quiet, for once, intimate and cozy, more inviting than its usual Animal House atmosphere. Jeanette's smile was as warm as the potbelly stove. The winsome girl was three, and she was looking at a book of Cajun fairy tales: *Jolie Blonde and the Three Heberts*. Her name was Lexi. She was the Jeanette's first grandchild and the first grandchild I met in Henderson. There would be many more. That day we slowly began talking and laughing, and the little marina store became, for a few moments, a girls' klatch instead of a hunting lodge. Jeanette has beautiful salt-and-pepper hair and a lilting, musical voice, its soothing tones reminiscent of my Grannie's, except with a Cajun accent. I loved her at once. I told her more about myself that day than I'd confided to a new friend in decades. Something about her kind face invited confidences.

The dock outside, with its snaggle-toothed smile of houseboats and population of hunters in gum boots and camouflage, suddenly looked and felt like Christmas. When I left the store, I hugged my Coke to myself and negotiated the Rube Goldberg-worthy labyrinth of decks and docks. I was happy. I had an invitation to visit the Latiolais home in Henderson on Christmas Eve. I flew back to the boat, feeling good about making a friend, my first. I had no idea at the time what a good friend.

Louisiana quickly became the perfect complement to our busy lives. Even persistent Atlanta editors couldn't reach me once I made it to the *Green Queen*, home free. For me, it was a floating refuge, not to mention a French fix on the cheap, a poor man's Provence. Didn't matter I'd never been to the real Provence; this was, in some ways, better. You could turn on the radio and hear the country standards we loved, Hank and Webb Pierce and Kitty Wells, only often on the air in southwest Louisiana they were being sung in French. The best version ever of that amazing song "Amazing Grace" is sung in French by Les Amies Louisianaises. They played "La Grace du Ciel" a lot during Christmas. Store windows boasted, "Nous parlons francais ici." And the flat-out decorating was definitely proof of French blood.

For Don, Henderson was about childhood, not so much about France. He said our Louisiana village reminded him of his hometown of Moss Point, Mississippi, in the 1940s. "Friends dropped by without calling or waiting for a formal invitation," he said. He thought such informality was a good thing. And certainly it was the case in Henderson. What's more, when the unannounced visitors came, you'd best have some Community Coffee handy and a pastry or two. And you never, ever got in a hurry; that was the first rule of Cajun hospitality. Conversation was a luxury that anyone could afford. In Henderson people might not have much. But they had time for you. And half of anything material they had was yours. If a pot was boiling on the stove you were expected, obligated, to stay and partake.

"Get down," Johnelle would demand in his marvelous Cajun accent. "Get down" meant, get out of the car, come inside, sit for a spell. Don't be in such an all-fired hurry.

And getting down was what we did a lot of. In Georgia I was constantly in a dither, finishing one column, worrying about the next. In the swamp, I was renewed, relaxed, and amazed at myself for feeling that way. The columns came more easily. I could always find something to write about. Once a column was done, I could forget about it.

Don was completely at home. He never saw any reason to feel like an outsider, though Cajuns have a reputation as an insular tribe. He would rush into the *Queen* with a story about a sheriff who had offered to peel the federal duck stamp off of his own hunting license to loan it to Don. Or a party planned as benefit to pay burial expenses for a man best known for dancing with a can of beer on his head. The *joie de vivre* that the Cajuns are famous for was abundantly evident in little Henderson, and we marveled that we had found it.

For thirteen years we would make the trip whenever the rest of life got too tedious or taxing. It was our emotional safety net, our affordable playground. It took the sting out of living near that octopus called Atlanta, and out of not being able to afford annual visits to France. It compensated nicely for never having seen the real Provence. It was an amazingly rich alternative, one we grew to depend on, and especially at Christmas.

# 18

# Home to the Hollow

I remember the exact day I decided for sure to leave Atlanta. The newspaper, in its wisdom, sent me to write the cutlines for a planned photo essay on a county fair. Cutlines.

Now I didn't mind the work, though writing cutlines is right up there with sharpening pencils. I love county fairs, in fact. But they were paying me more money than I'd ever thought it possible to earn working for a newspaper, and writing captions for photographs seemed an absurd waste of my creative energy. But, then, newspapers are known for squandering talent. It happens a lot, especially on large metro dailies.

What got to me that day was not the weird assignment, but the trip to complete it. I left my Carrollton home at 7 A.M., drove across Atlanta to an eastern suburb, headed back through the city and toward home. I wouldn't get there until 10 that night. Most of the day wasn't spent in the wonderful and musky cow barn where the photographer concentrated his lens, or out on the fairway that smelled of cotton candy and funnel cake and reminded me of my youth. And precious little time was spent at a desk in the newsroom writing cutlines. Oh, no. Most of the day was spent on the interstate in the Ford, sitting motionless, as state troopers cleared three lanes of a fatal accident involving a semi and several cars. Instead of being home to cook sup-per and relish the twilight before going to bed to get up to write yet another column, I was stuck in traffic.

"Stuck in traffic" was what people in Atlanta said when they failed to show up for a party, or arrived three hours late for an appointment. "Stuck in traffic" was the most believable excuse you could offer even when it wasn't true, when you'd really been lollygagging and hadn't gotten dressed early enough. Everyone had been there—instead of where he wanted to be—stuck in traffic, breathing gasoline fumes and pounding the dashboard, listening to radio helicopter traffic report-ers tell you alternate routes when it was too late to take them. I had been there myself hundreds of times, but that day I suddenly found it unbearable.

Life was too short to be stuck in traffic. That day when the inter-state finally was cleared, I cranked up my car but not quick enough to suit the man in the car behind me. He began honking his horn, as if I had been the reason we'd all been stuck for over an hour. He blew his horn, I thought of my peaceful home in the Mississippi hollow and the friendly folk of Henderson. That was the day I quietly planned my resignation.

The last week we were in Carrollton, Don happened to catch a wreck story on the local evening news, not a hard thing to catch. He talked about it for years afterwards. While troopers were investigat-ing yet another wreck with several fatalities, they happened to find an extra body in the tall grass on the roadside. Turns out, the seasoned body was a murder victim. Atlanta in a nutshell, Don would say. Traffic fatalities with an order of violence on the side.

I had dreamed of quitting the Atlanta newspaper many times. It was my new hobby, thinking about quitting. The first year I came so close to leaving that I rehearsed my speech. I'd ask my Mississippi friend Danny Barnes, who owned the Iuka ice plant and serviced all the region's convenience stores, for a job driving one of the ice trucks. "I'm hauling ass to Mississippi to haul ice," I could say in a final column. I had gotten my feelings hurt by the awful rants and reviews from readers who missed Lewis Grizzard. He'd been so popular they named a stretch of the interstate in his honor. At one point during his column career, there were bumper stickers that harkened to his multiple marriages and said "Honk If You've Never Been Married to Lewis Grizzard." When the complaint letters were vicious, I'd think to myself, "I didn't kill him. I was never even married to him."

I almost quit again my fourth year there when the newspaper changed its computer system and everyone in the newsroom was required to spend an entire week in computer class to learn yet another new system. I had started this business on a manual typewriter, and I'd learned at least twenty-five more technologies for typing a story over the years at different newspapers. With every technological leap, it seemed we spent less time on the writing and more coping with the mechanics. Some newspapers changed computers every time a salesman blew through town. I simply didn't know if I had another brain cell left to devote to the computer.

I did, of course. I struggled through the computer class along with everyone else.

But the most nerve-wracking moment had happened more recently. I was sick with worry and loss when the great Celestine Sibley died of cancer at age eighty-six. The editor told me he was moving my column to her old slot. God, no, I thought, not again. The *AJC* was putting me in the place left vacant by *another* dead icon. As much as I had admired her, I didn't want to be put in the thankless position of trying to replace her. I had reason to worry. Celestine was more popular in Georgia than any sports figure, politician, or movie star. She had been given what amounted to a state funeral, and the governor declared a day in her honor.

But this time when my column ran on hallowed ground, I wasn't an unknown quantity. This time, readers seemed happy to see a replacement. Maybe Celestine just had a more polite following than did Grizzard. Or maybe it was because we were both women.

I had managed to stay and keep writing for seven years, and my column now had a following of its own. After seven years it should have. The work never got any easier, but at least now readers, some of them, appreciated my efforts. I might have settled in for the duration. On good days, I could imagine it happening. The money was amazing, the newspaper liberal. Its owner liked me, or at least she liked my writing; I never actually met her. I might have worked at the *AJC* till I was eighty-six, though whenever I'd seen Celestine in the hallway I got the heebie-jeebies. It was like seeing the Ghost of Christmas Future, myself as a truly old woman still having to produce four columns a week to eat.

Don and I loved our house on the Little Tallapoosa River and could have been happy staying put, dropping our canoe into the river at every opportunity. Except for the nightmarish growth all around us. Atlanta was headed our way, like that red menace of 1950s cinema, The Blob. Every time we drove to town and back there seemed to be a new subdivision in a cow pasture. A cell tower with blinking lights went up in the swampy area just beyond our woods. Mostly, though, it was the traffic that bedeviled. The logistics of getting around that monstrous metropolitan cancer called Atlanta wasted too much of my life. I didn't mind putting in eight, even ten hours a day to the job if it improved what I wrote. I'd done that and far worse. But I hated wasting time in the car. I was nearing fifty, my priorities had changed, and Don had retired from teaching. I wanted, desperately, to go home. And home, to me, meant Mississippi.

And so we did.

Don was not long on compliments. He thought I should know and remember certain things, and that he shouldn't have to repeat the obvious. He loved me. I knew it. End of story. If he told you once that were pretty, you were supposed to remember that. He'd let you know if he changed his mind. If he told you he liked your writing once, that was enough, he figured. It was a consistent belief with Don, not just how he dealt with needy me. He was appalled, for instance, at the way modern parents praised children constantly in an effort to reinforce their self-esteem. "It's been shown that hard-core criminals have the most self-esteem," he would note. He was a man of few words, and precious few of those were compliments.

It surprised and thrilled me, then, when he praised me for quitting the Atlanta paper. Most of my friends and family thought I was making a huge mistake and said so. "It shows real character to turn your back on all that money," Don said. I relished the rare lavish compliment and still do. It might have been his highest ever.

I've never known anyone less materialistic. Once when Chelsey was small we visited Don at his spartan Smith Lake trailer. After she returned home, Chelsey sat drawing an elaborate picture. Sheila asked if it were a thank you for Reeree, as Chelsey called me. "It's for Don," the child said. "He doesn't have much."

It wasn't like I quit work altogether. I would write one column a week. I would still have my syndication salary—the column was distributed by King Features Syndicate of New York—but that was less than one-tenth what I'd made at the newspaper. Mostly we would live on Don's teacher's pension and Social Security. I would, if we married, be able to have his insurance. So we married. Not the most romantic of reasons to legalize our relationship eight years into it, but a darn good one.

We were, even before I quit my job, making a lot of trips between Fishtrap Hollow in Mississippi and the Georgia house. Don was working on closing in a back porch that would give us more room in the little Mississippi farmhouse. Whenever we made the drive, we passed through the Alabama town of Moulton. I always took notice, mostly because I'd once had a front page story with a Moulton dateline. I never forgot a front page byline. Back in the early 1980s, I had covered the controversy that erupted when county officials had refused to allow a statue of native son Jesse Owens on the courthouse lawn. Track star Jesse Owens had singlehandedly humiliated Hitler, but that didn't mean the black gold medalist belonged with the Confederate soldiers, or so the powers-that-be decided. A small group of black Masons in the nearby countryside paid for the statue. They were proud to give it a home. Before it could be unveiled, hoodlums in a pickup truck toppled it. Finally, a decade later, the county embraced the statue and the idea of Jesse Owens as hero, putting a park and museum at the rather remote site.

Math isn't my subject, but I bet if you put a pencil to the number of stories I've reported and written over the years, the ones with a racial angle would amount to over 90 percent. "If you scratch hard enough," one wise editor said once, "every story in the South has a racial angle."

Because of its geography, between our two towns, I decided Moulton was as good a place as any to marry. Moulton certainly had no monopoly on racist leaders. I phoned the circuit judge to make an appointment. I said something like, "We're old and not religious. We want your shortest wedding." He laughed.

The day of the "ceremony" we dressed. I insisted on dignity and wore a plain gray dress I usually reserved for the occasional speeches that columnists are forced to make. Don wore his navy blue blazer, a necktie—a true concession since he'd sworn never to wear another after retirement—and gray pants. We had our dog Maxi with us in the red pickup truck, and I put a garbage bag between me and the hairy canine to keep my good dress fresh. We arrived in Moulton a little early and decided to go eat a barbecue-stuffed potato at a favorite restaurant in the area, Classical Fruits and Barbecue. It was run by an Auburn couple, and Don and I always had trouble passing it up. Dignity wouldn't be abetted by a stomach growling from hunger.

I couldn't help contrasting my second marriage day with my first. On my first I'd been worried about everything, especially appearances. This time I was more comfortable with myself, and there was a total lack of pretentious trappings. We didn't even exchange rings, though Don would get me a gold band the next Christmas.

After the stuffed potato, it was marrying time. The friendly judge laughed when he saw us. "You're not that old," he said. But he honored my request. It was the briefest ceremony in the history of true love.

Minutes later we were married in the eyes of the law. We'd been committed to one another a lot longer in our own minds, and we would always celebrate another anniversary. I have to strain to remember my actual wedding date for official documents.

Walking down the courthouse steps, I asked a stranger walking up to take our photograph. He obliged. It's the only picture of our wedding day, and we look as happy as you can at an Alabama courthouse in stuffy dress clothes. But then we usually did look happy in those days. How many people find love so late? How many couples agree on almost everything, especially simple pleasures like porch-sitting and Hank Williams music and barbecue-stuffed potatoes? We didn't need diamonds or a Lexus. We needed one another. Don had not galloped into my life on a white stallion as Sir Galahad. He had trotted up on a dependable Quarter Horse, more Gus McRae than Galahad.

The past Christmas a neighbor's goats had gotten loose in the hollow and eaten my nandinas down to their last red berry. I was devastated along with the shrubs. So Don spent several weeks of his summer building a fence around the front yard of the old farmhouse, making each picket on his table saw by hand. I kidded him about the domesticity of that scene: man building picket fence. Though he bristled at most convention, he didn't seem to mind the ribbing this time. Don was the easiest person to get along with I'd ever known. And with the release from newspaper and daily deadline bondage for the first time in over thirty years, I was becoming a little easier to live with, too.

# 19

# Madeleine

When I woke from surgery, Don was there, standing by my bedside looking worried. I was in the oldest continuously operating hospital in Europe, possibly the world, Paris's legendary Hotel-Dieu, located on the Ile de la Cite, next to Notre Dame.

Hotel-Dieu, translated, means God's Mansion. And it was a literal mansion, with manicured gardens inside of a spacious courtyard, and imposing hallways with portraits of famous surgeons and scientists who had worked there over the centuries. Saint Landry started the hospital back in 651, so, when the question arose, I figured the facility had done an appendectomy or two. In the Middle Ages, they draped black cloth across the entrances to signal there was no more room for Black Plague victims. And though fire had wiped out the place more than once, the existing 1800s architecture was impressive enough. I wouldn't be able to appreciate any of its beauty until I left the place.

"I feel funny," I had said the night before at a bus stop near the Hotel de Suez where we were staying with our buddy and true gourmet, John Bedford. We'd just had an obscenely rich dinner of rabbit with cream sauce, not to mention three kinds of cheeses and a chocolate dessert. Something wasn't sitting right. I first dismissed the rumblings as the obvious: too much food.

By 3 A.M., I knew, somehow, my appendix was about to burst. Don't ask me how I knew, I just knew. I had never been in so much pain. Don asked the concierge to call a taxi, and we headed to the nearest "Urgency," or French emergency room, which just happened to be the one at the legendary Hotel-Dieu. I writhed in pain on a table for a few minutes until a nurse shot me full of something, I didn't much care what. Moments later, an MRI proved right my gut hunch about my gut. A kind doctor who spoke fluent English came over and told me what I already knew. I was about to have my appendix taken out in Paris. Not exactly as romantic as leaving your heart in San Francisco, but a body part left in a favorite city, nonetheless.

"You should not worry," he said. "We have very fine surgeons here."

"Oh, I'm not worried," I said. "I'd rather have surgery here than in the U.S."

The doctor probably didn't know what I was talking about—I was too weak to explain—and I'm certain he thought my reaction strange for an ailing American tourist. But I'd read enough to know the French health system had to be an improvement on the American medical scene. The World Health Organization, in fact, ranked France at the tiptop in terms of affordable and good care. And everything that happened to me the next few days bore out that official judgment.

Three days and nights later, after the MRI and emergency surgery and heaven knows how much pain medicine, my total bill was $3,000. The MRI alone would have cost that much in the U.S. In our pidgin French Don and I repeatedly tried to tell the surgeon and other doctors that we had insurance, and that we would and could pay the bill. To a person, the doctors waved their hands in dismissal and said, "Don't worry about that. It is not my concern. Let's get you well."

Our French friend Marie-Lu came to the hospital several times to translate for Don. The doctor who had explained things to me seemed to be the only staff member there who spoke much English. I didn't care. Medical terminology is Greek to me in any language. I found it comforting to be in the dark about procedure. At night I'd hear a team of nurses whispering in lovely French and see them using pen lights to check my IV. They tried their best not to wake patients.

In an attempt at cheerfulness after the surgery, I'd tell all the nurses, maids, doctors, and even the patient in the bed next to me, "Je suis Madeline." I'd grown up reading Ludwig Bemelmans's story about the little French orphan who had her appendix out and made all the other orphan girls jealous by showing off her fine new scar. *And all the little girls cried, "Boohoo, we want to have our appendix out, too!"*

"Je suis Madeline," I said again and again to anyone who would listen, but to absolutely no reaction. I thought it was a clever allusion. One nurse looked puzzled and glanced at my chart. She must have thought the drugs had made me forget my own name.

"Je suis Madeline," I said to Marie-Lu, who sweetly asked, "Who is Madeline?"

Because Marie-Lu is one of the best-read people I know in any language, I suddenly realized that the Madeline classics must not be so familiar in France. Or, as Marie-Lu said to my true dismay that day, "Never heard of it." I mailed her a copy of the *American* classic later.

Don and John did their best to keep me upbeat with lots of visits and news from outside. They were an odd couple, standing there awkwardly at the end of my hospital bed, looking worried and confused. John was tall and bald, Don short with thick beautiful hair. Through the haze of drugs I thought John looked like a mortician and Don a priest, comprising a team of ghouls come to give me last rites and bury me.

I think the whole business was much harder on Don than me. The French have the rather reasonable policy of no overnight guests in the hospital room, so Don was spared that duty. But during visitors' hours he came and sat. And sat. I insisted that he eat some more great meals for me, and finally, but only after visiting hours were over each day, he did. John and Don dutifully reported back on the restaurants and menus they sampled while I rested in God's Mansion. I couldn't help but notice there was red wine on all the lunch trays in the hospital, though I was on a drip diet of another kind for most of my stay.

I dearly love the French meringues that grow like mushrooms in all the little Paris bakeries. I resolved to buy one as soon as I was released. I would get one in each flavor and subsist on a meringue diet until we flew home. When finally I left the hospital, Don at my side, we took a taxi to the Hotel de Suez. It was a glorious "homecoming." Don had hung an Eiffel Tower mobile over the bed, and John brought me the largest meringue I've ever seen, an almond one.

We had been on our way to Belgium via Paris when my appendix altered our plans. We were all set to swap homes with a Belgian couple, Mia and Jos, in the small town of Tielt, near Bruges. Two years earlier I had discovered a house-swapping organization called HomeLink that helps teachers, writers, and other middle-class folks travel on a budget. The idea is to swap homes, and even automobiles, with people in other countries that you'd like to visit.

After I discovered that there are a lot of French-speaking people the world over who want to visit Cajun Louisiana, I went a little nuts arranging swaps. We had bought a little Cajun cottage in Henderson when it became clear how much time we'd be spending there. For a while we had both the *Green Queen* and a house, but that required a little too much maintenance. Or, as sensible Don put it, "too many toilets to fix." We sold the boat that had begun our Louisiana adventure and were a little sad. But having a real house and a yard in which to plant azaleas eased the sting.

Our first exchange was with a young Normandy couple with a son. The husband and wife were teachers and lived in a renovated seventeenth-century hunting lodge on spacious and bucolic grounds in some of the most calendar-worthy countryside I've ever seen. There were more castles than trailers, hydrangeas blue as swimming pool bottoms. Each small town paid for employees to water the flowers in boxes on every bridge and hanging from every municipal building. I found it hard to believe the French teachers wanted to swap their palatial estate for our Henderson house—and in August. But they did. After negotiating the exchange, Don said I tried my best to talk them out of it.

"I notice in my reading that the median temperature in Normandy in July and August is seventy-two degrees," I emailed to Frederick, the husband. "I'm afraid it often gets to the high nineties in Louisiana in August, and the humidity makes it seem hotter."

I dutifully told them about the mosquitoes, the litter on the Louisiana highways, the vicious pit bulls in the yard next to ours. The wonder is they came at all after my full disclosure campaign. I wanted no unpleasant surprises for our first French visitors. I supervised the construction of a new brick walk—in case of rain, which often flooded our Henderson yard. I insisted Don hire a mechanic to check out his Nissan, our official swap car. It was making a funny but harmless noise when put in reverse. The mechanic said the noise really didn't matter, but several hundred dollars later it was gone. That helped my feelings; I now was certain that our visitors Frederick and Marie would not hear the grinding sound and worry, even if needlessly. I was on a roll. I enlisted every friend and relative I knew who owed us any kind of favor, insisting that they plan parties and entertain the French guests. I was in a dither, all in the name of France.

The summer of that first house swap, 2003, was also the summer of the fluke European heat wave when seventy-five thousand French people died from the record hot temperatures. Hit especially hard were the elderly in city apartments without air-conditioning. It was hotter that year in Normandy than in Henderson, Louisiana, believe it or not. Our first two weeks in Normandy we wore jackets. Then we began shedding clothes like Blaze Starr as the temperature climbed higher and higher.

I kept remembering the photos we had exchanged before making the swap official. HomeLink suggests you make your home seem real to potential house guests by mailing them plenty of photographs. Everyone chooses flattering ones, of course. Marie had mailed to me family photographs from the Christmas before. There was snow in the Normandy cow pastures. In one photo, Little Corentin, her son, sat beneath a live Christmas tree in the fantastic main room with its ancient beams and stocked bookshelves. When the August heat became so unbearable we quit touring, quit going outside at all, I tried to remember those Christmas pictures and make myself cooler. When the little Renault overheated on the way to Mont Saint Michel, I closed my eyes and concentrated on the scene in a photograph that had shown their gate wrapped in snow and Christmas garland.

So I need not have worried. At least not about Frederick and Marie. At least not about heat.

The French had a ball in workaday Henderson. There were parties, cookouts, swamp cruises, and sailboat adventures. Friends from three states helped entertain the family, and I'm quite certain international relations, queasy because of the Gulf War, were helped in some small way.

As wonderful as we found Normandy, getting there, for once, was more fun than being in France. And a lot cooler. Don and I had always wanted to take a freighter somewhere, anywhere. I had read about writers taking advantage of the solitude on board to finish their manuscripts. It was said Alex Haley wrote most of his *Roots* while on a working boat. You couldn't have paid either of us to book a normal pleasure cruise. "It makes me nervous for people to wait on me," Don had said in his succinct way. He spoke for us both, as usual.

I went online and found a German freighter company that rented their extra cabins, mostly former officers' quarters freed up when computerized equipment cut the officer ranks. When you book a ride on a container ship, nothing is exact. Don and I were to be at the Port of Savannah, Georgia, on or about July 4. We'd wait in a nearby motel for a call from the captain who would tell us when and where to board.

From there we would sail to Valencia, Spain, and then board a train to Barcelona. From Barcelona we would take another train to Paris, where we'd catch still another train to Briouze, Normandy, the town with a station nearest Frederick and Marie's home. At the station we'd find—we hoped—the Renault they were swapping for our Nissan. They had mailed us the car keys earlier.

If you're going to make a trip, make a trip.

We had to present a doctor's letter to our ship's captain, a testimonial that we were in good health. We also had to spring for insurance that would pay for any delays that an unexpected illness might cause the freighter company.

To avoid leaving our car parked in Georgia for two months, Buba and Annie drove us to Savannah, where we spent three pleasant but anxious days looking around that moss-draped city. We were eager to be underway and to begin our greatest adventure ever. On July 4th, Independence Day, we watched fireworks over the Savannah River and anticipated the departure. The next morning the call came. We climbed up the ladder-like gangplank and onto the freighter. Our cabin was larger than our Henderson house, with a foyer, a main room, bathroom and bedroom. We could have thrown parties or had dances, only we were the only passengers traveling on the *MS California Senator* with its German officers and Filipino crew.

We hurried aboard only to wait. And wait. It took hours for the crew to load the containers, 80 percent of them empty, that the boat would carry to Europe, and to get ready to finally cast off. On the return trip, all of the containers were full, a graphic illustration of this country's trade deficit.

I fell asleep beneath a snow-white down comforter before the ship ever moved. I was snoring when we left the Port of Savannah, missing the sights and lights of River Street where we'd been walking just the day before. I have never slept so well or so much as I did on that freighter, its diesel engines humming a throaty lullaby. When I wasn't sleeping, I wrote, or read. We took meals with the officers, and only at the prescribed meal times. If you missed the appointed time, you didn't eat. The food was mostly German fare, delicious and plentiful. I'm ambivalent about most soups, but the ones on board were amazing, meals unto themselves. Soup was just the first course. The crew ate in another dining hall where we were not invited. Dozens of pairs of flip-flops would be left outside the crew dining room during meals.

Many mornings our Filipino steward, Simplicio, would knock at our cabin door and announce, "We have passed into another time zone. You should set your clocks ahead one hour." There would be no jet lag this trip to France, as we eased day by day into European time.

Because we were the only passengers, Don and I were treated royally. We had our own deck to watch the sun set over the Atlantic each and every afternoon. We had use of the officers' swimming pool, which no officers ever used. It was filled with fresh sea water every day. On Sunday, we were invited by the captain, Ingolf Hahn, and the chief engineer to "tea" in the dining room. We dreaded the fancy-sounding, if customary, ceremony, but we went anyway to be polite. There was tea, all right, on linen cloths in a silver service, but also several bottles of fine wine and a German chocolate cake big as a hat box. By the end of tea, it didn't matter that the two officers spoke little English and we knew one word of German: "Kaput." Lubed by alcohol, we were all communicating fluently.

Our snip of German came in handy. One night, in the middle of the Atlantic, sleeping like drunk babies, we were awakened by the sound of silence. The diesel engine had shut down. For several hours after that we could hear attempts to get it going again, sort of like a giant motorcycle being gunned by an impatient biker. The next day Don asked our captain what had happened to the engine. "Kaput," said the captain, using the one word we understood. We understood.

After that quiet night I worried about what would happen if the freighter had engine trouble that could not be remedied at sea. Would we be towed back to the U.S.—what I feared the most—or on to Europe? It depended, the engineer explained, on which continent we were closer to at the time.

We were greatly relieved once we passed the halfway point.

You have to like your own company to make a freighter trip enjoyable. You have to love solitude, and reading. You have to love one another. At times I'd look across the cabin at Don, his nose in some book, and think but not say, "I wish this trip would last forever." It was as close to perfect happiness as I've ever known. On a ship, in the ocean, alone with the man you love and lots of books, steaming toward France. Utter bliss.

"I think I'll live on a freighter instead of in a nursing home when I'm old," Don said one day, doing the math. We were paying about one hundred dollars a day each for the passage. "It would cost about the same amount."

The first land we saw after nine days at sea was the Strait of Gibraltar. The drama of that sighting will be with me till I die. I knew then how the astronauts must feel when they reenter earth's orbit. You are relieved and sad at the same time. It meant we were closer to my beloved France, but that our sea voyage was ending.

Everyone, including the seasoned captain, remarked about the smooth passage we had. There was no rolling, no crashing of waves, no seasickness. I've seen small lakes more tumultuous than the Atlantic Ocean in the two weeks we traveled. Don, I think, was almost disappointed. He loves wave action and kept looking longingly at the straps that would hold our chairs and other cabin appointments in place if a storm came up. I was happy enough to be spared that part of the adventure.

We caught a ride into town with one of the officers and bought gifts for all of our new freighter friends, from Simplicio to Captain Hahn. Both Don and I hated to leave the freighter. It had been a compact, quiet, and satisfying world unto itself, a suspended paradise where time has little meaning. Again and again friends would ask, "What did you do all that time in the middle of the ocean?" We would look at one another and smile.

We had no way of knowing that this trip, our greatest holiday ever, would mark the last completely carefree summer of our lives. By the same time the next year, Don's chest would have been cut open, his big and kind heart stopped for repair, and temporarily mended. After the bypass, he recovered quickly and well and went back to splitting firewood, hunting ducks, and living his life. But he was no longer a candidate for traveling across the ocean on a slow boat.

# 20

# Laissez Les Bon Temps Rouler

on did anything he could to keep me happy at Christmas. If I were happy, he was free to duck hunt. And then he, too, was happy. He was more passionate about being in the Henderson swamp hunting ducks than almost anything else in life. He didn't deer hunt at all. Deer, he said, looked too much like dogs. He liked to go dove hunting once or twice in the fall, and he often shot squirrels for what he called his "varmint stew." But it was the duck hunting that got his blood boiling, the Louisiana swamp scene that most moved him.

So, come fall, our favorite season, he'd get out his old shotgun, carefully clean it and start making preparations. It was about the same time I started planning "our" Christmas, though he'd have been happy with Vienna sausages from a can and a holiday card from a friend taped to the door. What he did to prepare for Christmas, he did to please me. And he did a lot. He would haul decorations down from the attic, screw Santa to the front gate, try to loop lights over the highest spruce, cut a cedar for the porch from the railroad right of way, lasso Rudolph if it meant keeping me happy at Christmas.

"Are you depressed yet?" he'd sometimes ask in a panic if I'd chance to frown in concentration. He believed that anyone half smart who indulged in Christmas eventually got burnt. Disappointed and depressed. If I got disappointed and depressed, he got disappointed and depressed. And it would have meant his having to take time out from the hunt to get me over what Celestine Sibley used to call "the down yonders." And he couldn't stand to see me sad.

I understood where he was coming from. I really did. It was true that an inordinate number of sad things happened at Christmas, or around Christmas. Or maybe depressing things just seemed worse at Christmas. The first funeral I ever attended, for instance, that of my Uncle Bill, my father's brother, was Christmas week. His widow, Beulah Helen, was such a pathetic sight that I agreed in a family cemetery and a weak moment to spend the next summer with her. I was sixteen.

Aunt Beulah was supervisor at a sewing plant in south Georgia, a tough "foreman" feared by the working women. And most of the employees in the "sewing room," as everyone called it, were women. But at night the fierce "Miss Beulah" who broke up fights amongst the seamstresses melted into a soft puddle of widowhood. She was scared to stay in her own home alone. So she took me up on my offer and got me a summer job as a pattern bundler.

While I imagined my friends back home were dating and water skiing and polishing their toenails, I was walking an assembly line in an un-air conditioned sewing plant, picking up a right arm, a left arm, a bodice and the rest of the parts that when sewn together would become a fuzzy housecoat. I would bundle the pattern pieces as quickly as possible, trying to "make production," whatever that was. Thanks to hard work, the days went by quickly. I even made several friends, joining them for the thirty minutes we were given to eat our sack lunches beneath the shade of a tree in the factory parking lot.

The south Georgia nights were much, much longer. At night I'd listen to the tree frogs and the sound of my aunt crying. My being there didn't much help her troubled mind. Whenever a storm threatened, we'd load up in her car and go a quarter of a mile down the dirt road to spend the night with her daughter and son-in-law. Whenever she had a bad day, we'd load up and go to the daughter's. We spent at least as much time with the daughter that summer as we did in her home. I guess a visiting teenager wasn't much insurance against bad lightning and raw grief.

Christmas is the time you miss the missing the most. The list of dead relatives and friends grows from Christmas to Christmas, if you are lucky enough to grow old yourself. Don's one concession to the holiday for years was an expensive long-distance phone call to friends in faraway places. Each year his forehead would furrow as he'd make another mark through a name in his worn address book. After cell phones became common and long-distance calling cheap, he complained his one tradition had lost all meaning. People were now calling long-distance as frequently and nonchalantly as they used to yoo-hoo across the yard.

Along with trying to ward off seasonal depression, Don would agonize over what gift to buy me. That was another thing he hated about the holidays: shopping. "I'm not stupid," he said rather defensively before our first Christmas together. "I know women like jewelry."

But, as I pointed out to him three rings and several pairs of earrings later, you can only wear so much jewelry. After he gave me a gold wedding band every other bauble seemed superfluous. So Don's gifts to me grew more practical. One year he picked out luggage with wheels. The low point was a sewing machine, and he saw the disappointment in my eyes.

"But you said you wanted to learn to sew," he protested.

"No, I said I wish I *knew how* to sew," I corrected. "There's a difference."

One year in a stylish shop in Breaux Bridge, Louisiana, Don discovered the Lampe Berger, a century-old Paris invention that not only perfumed the air with hundreds of different and delicious scents, but also served as disinfectant. The lamps came in all shapes, patterns and sizes, and increased in value over the years. I loved the lamp and its French history, its Parisian blend of practicality and beauty. Don, ecstatic over his success, bought me another one the next Christmas.

Don and I now stayed in Louisiana from Thanksgiving through January. I wrote the column only for syndication, so there was no pressure to be any certain place at any given time. We began a routine that always, always took into consideration the duck hunting season, which, of course, put us in Henderson for the holidays. And it took some doing to get depressed in Henderson, even at Christmas. For one thing, you could look out the front window and see working people with much more to be depressed about. They'd been laid off from the Fruit of the Loom plant relocated to Honduras, or lost a limb on an offshore rig, or had an automobile repossessed during the night. And they were managing. They were stringing Christmas lights from pillar to post, playing the happiest music in the world on their portable boom boxes, cooking up amazing things in pots big as Volkswagens. Where did we get off complaining?

For the most part, Don stayed in the swamp. I bought him a Moon Beam clock, which flashed a yellow light instead of bleating an alarm to wake you. He would slip from our warm bed and make coffee for his thermos and put on several layers of clothing before heading toward the levee. Sometimes I went with him in his skiff in the late afternoon to put out his decoys for the next morning. I found new enthusiasm for the chore when Don described the process as "just like decorating a Christmas tree." The plastic ducks, not unlike tree ornaments, were spaced carefully apart so they'd look real to their brethren in the air.

The local area's abundance of live music and good food was extraordinary. Don and I savored both. For seven years straight we drove to the old Liberty Theater in Eunice for a Hank Williams tribute staged on a Saturday during the holidays. It was Hank like we'd never heard him. D. L. Menard, sometimes billed as the Cajun Hank Williams, sang the plaintive standards in his heavy accent. An imitator named Hugh Harris—prison guard at Angola by day, Hank by night—sounded and looked, except for his short height, like the lanky real thing.

There was a name for the music we both liked: roots music. We liked old country, traditional Cajun, the blues. We didn't care for the heavily orchestrated sound that seemed to dominate so much popular music. Or, as Don said, quoting Woody Guthrie, "If you use more than three chords, you're showing off."

We'd become friends with Helene Boudreaux, a swamp chanteuse who called herself the Catahoula Cajun Truck Driving Mama. Retired after a back injury from driving the big rigs, Helene checked out a library video that taught her to play the guitar. The singing came naturally. And often. Whenever we asked, Helene would appear at our house and sing her heart out for supper. Don often sang with her, his voice world-weary and Mississippi soft. He'd play the same old Gibson guitar a girlfriend had given him when he was sixteen. Live music in Henderson was like pizza, then. They'd deliver it to your home.

Speaking of food, I did precious little cooking in Louisiana. That would have been coals to Newcastle for certain. There was always yet another po-boy stand we hadn't tried, or a plate lunch shack; they grew up like thistle in the fields. Don and I had seen a Memphis billboard once that advertised a Mississippi casino buffet. On the billboard was a photograph on an obscenely obese couple, with a quote in a cartoon balloon coming from their smacking lips: "This is an *awesome* restaurant!" Whenever we'd head toward a Cajun restaurant that tempted us to overeat, Don would say, "This is an awesome restaurant." We'd laugh, pledge to do better in north Mississippi where you can't get good bread on a bet and it's much easier to diet.

Johnelle would simply phone us when their holiday meals were ready, and we'd belly up with the rest of the extended family. That first Christmas Eve invitation from Jeanette so long ago seemed to have been perpetual. And once you've sat there while the family's matriarch distributes the Christmas money on Christmas Eve, you might as well return the next day for the rest of the gift swap.

Jeanette's main Christmas meal was at noon, straight up, except for the times that there were so many people we ate in shifts. One year we broke bread with a murderer, a fact Johnelle matter-of-factly pointed out when the man had said his thanks and left. We had wondered who the quiet stranger at the table was, but assumed he spoke only French and therefore didn't engage us in conversation. That often happened with older Cajuns. Turns out, he was Johnelle's mother's brother-in-law, who had beaten her sister to death and served time for manslaughter.

Everyone called Johnelle's mother "Toot." "The priest said we should forgive him," Toot explained. "So I did."

The meals were amazing with or without murderers. If you happened to stop at Jeanette's on a Wednesday, say, and she had cooked meatballs and rice and asked you to eat, which she would, it would be the best meatballs and rice you've ever put in your mouth. Cajun cooks use the "holy trinity"—chopped onion, garlic, and bell pepper—

to season everything. So everything is good, and a walk through any Henderson neighborhood smells like heaven would if Julia Child were God. But for holidays, Jeanette really let loose. There would be three kinds of meat, rice dressing, sweet potatoes, potato salad, and every kind of dessert that the local baker T-Sue offers. "Wretched excess," Don would complain in jest. Before we were done with the Christmas meal, Johnelle would be lovingly describing the seafood gumbo planned for New Year's. We were, of course, invited.

It was one thing the Cajun culture had in common with my south Georgia Cracker culture. We valued food above almost anything else, and felt a need, as Don often said, "to plan our next meal."

Don never hunted on Christmas day. He let the hunters who weren't retired and off during the week have the lake on holidays and most weekends. So to kill time between Cajun meals we often drove through the countryside looking at Christmas lights. Plentiful and elaborate as decorations were, they were upstaged by the intentional fires burning the sugar cane back to the stalks in the fields, a glorious sight despite their negative environmental impact. Nothing's prettier than cane fields burning in the distance on that flat, endless Louisiana landscape. Not even the holly on your own front door.

21

# Petit Papa Noel

The last Christmas of his life, I left Don alone in the swamp. I went to Paris with girlfriends. I was home two days before Christmas, if you are into technicalities. But I was gone for much of December, the part of the Christmas season that's better than the actual day itself. Upon returning, I had jet lag so bad that I wasn't good for much.

Don didn't mind my going to France without him, or if he did he never let on. He encouraged my trip, in fact. He said he was perfectly happy, staying behind and minding the dogs and hunting the ducks. By now we had three dogs and somebody had to care for them. There was our spoiled yellow Labrador named Mabel, a pound puppy named Boozoo, and a happen-up mutt named Hank. Keeping the trio was just about a full-time job. And the last part of my trip revolved around a Bordeaux wedding, which Don insisted wasn't really his thing. So I left him.

I phoned home every night from Paris. Part of what made our rental apartment such a sweet deal was free calls to the U.S. Though he wasn't much for talking on the telephone to anyone, Don always acted interested in hearing about what we'd done each day. "As long

as you're having a good time," he would say before good-night. And
he meant it.

I was having a wonderful time. I was with my friends Pat and
Beth and my kindred spirit Annie. Annie's Buba, Don's brother, had
died the February before, and everyone thought the trip to France
would help Annie, who was valiantly struggling. She had the look of a
drowning woman who keeps gripping the side of the pool but cannot
pull herself up. It was Annie's great-niece, Laura, who was marrying
a Frenchman in Bordeaux.

Annie did seem buoyed by the Paris lights and endless sights. This
will get her out of the pool, I naively thought.

The amazingly spacious apartment I had rented was only a block
from the prettiest and oldest square in Paris, Place de Vosges. We'd
been on the ground for about thirty minutes before Annie and I
found a florist across the street who sold live Christmas trees. We
hustled our tree in its "hairnet" up the narrow stairs to our apartment.
We decorated with French ornaments that we could take home as
souvenirs for friends and relatives. We used scarves and earrings and
gloves—anything that added a touch of color and fun. We sprang
for two strings of lights, which, in France, have circular cords and are
dropped over the top of the tree like a trap. It was beautiful, same as
all Christmas trees.

The apartment's velvet portieres were red, as was the upholstery on
the sofas and chairs. The place had a Christmas feel to it even before
we bought the tree. Soon I found a children's Christmas CD at a street
market, and any time we were in the apartment, day or night, we played
"Petit Papa Noel," a beautiful mix of carols sung, of course, in French.
We went to sleep each night with the music playing. By the time we
left Paris for Bordeaux, we could all sing the words to the title song.

It had been another frilly dream of mine to see Paris at Christmas. Like everything else French, Christmas there lived up to all expectations. Even mine. There were lights on the Galerie Lafayette department store in the design of Notre Dame's Rose Window. There were live Christmas trees grouped at street corners, and Metro stops done up in blue satin bows. There were cases of wine hanging from trees on Montmartre. The Eiffel Tower was dressed in blue lights, and it took my breath away to round a corner and see the shockingly beautiful electric art. The blue reminded me of my mother's candles in our little subdivision house those Christmases long ago. Whether in an Alabama ranch house, Elvis Presley's Graceland, or on an iconic Paris landmark, blue wears well at Christmas.

The Bordeaux wedding, like Paris, was an endless pageant of color and beauty. The bride looked like a movie star—it is *not* true that all brides are beautiful; ditto babies—and the groom and his family were as gorgeous as you expect the French to be. All of us, the entire wedding party, boarded a chartered bus to a chateau in the countryside for a reception that lasted late into the December night. Champagne and wine flowed, a band played, everyone danced and, late in the evening, Annie kissed a gorgeous Frenchman named Philippe right on the lips, though she didn't remember having done so the next day. The party was that good. I knew Don would have liked this part of the trip, the part he'd said he was most glad to avoid.

Don was at the New Orleans airport to greet us after our hectic and crowded flight home. He looked tired, but then he often did during duck season. When a night owl such as Don has to rise at 5 A.M. and can't manage to nap during the day, he's often a little out of it. I'd kid him about being a "zombie" for the duration of duck season.

But it was I who was the zombie that Christmas. I had a hard time getting over the trip. I was tired, irritable, and experienced the worst lag I'd ever known. After our Christmas in Paris, I couldn't quite get up for decorating a tree with only two days left till Christmas. For the first time in my life, I let it slide. Don seemed surprised, but said he didn't mind.

I can't for the life of me remember much about our last Christmas. And I have tried. God knows I have tried. I know we ate with Jeanette and Johnelle at noon on Christmas, as usual, and that I gave Don a special knife from France as his main gift. We drank eggnog with whiskey and ate oyster po-boys on Christmas Eve, which was tradition. Don always fried the oysters. He was good at it. When he was young, Don's mother had fried oysters for him every morning for breakfast one year when she and his father made a short-lived attempt at operating a seafood restaurant on the coast. Our po-boys were wonderful; I remember that much. For some reason I even kept the plastic pint container that said "Joey Oysters, Amite, Louisiana." I was glad later.

But I don't remember certain things, and it tortures me. I don't remember if we went for a ride to see the lights, for instance. I don't think we did. I didn't have the energy. I don't remember if Don went hunting the day after Christmas. I don't think that he did. He didn't have the energy. Unlike all the duck seasons before, he had missed a few days, alternating between resting and hunting. He never admitted to feeling bad, but said he might only go every other day until the hunting got better. Our freezer already was full of ducks wrapped in aluminum foil, anyhow, fowl killed by Don, cleaned by Don, to be cooked by Don.

Near the end of our Louisiana respite, in January, we talked about the possibility of selling the Henderson house. We didn't want to. But it was becoming too expensive to keep two houses, even though both were paid for, in such a rotten economy. Insurance had gone sky high after Hurricane Katrina. Taxes kept rising. Twice during the fall we'd had to make rushed trips down to clean up after hurricanes Gustav and Ike. The globe was getting warmer, and we weren't getting younger. We sadly decided that we might have spent our last Christmas in Henderson, at least as residents. Don said he could still drive down and hunt a time or two each year, but maybe we wouldn't plan our lives around it anymore. We agreed to return in the early spring and talk to a real estate agent about the state of the market and to determine a reasonable asking price for our yellow cottage.

Our last Henderson trip together was in February 2009. Marie-Lu from Paris was visiting John Bedford in New Orleans. We drove from Henderson to New Orleans for the day to see her and to have a meal. We sat around a big table in the French Quarter and shared tamales and small talk. Don hated the New Orleans traffic and attendant confusion, but he loved Marie-Lu. He promised to take her duck hunting the next year. We couldn't spend the night because our dogs were back in Henderson, home alone. By nightfall we were back in our own bed with our dogs splayed out around us.

It was a short Louisiana trip, but we both enjoyed it. There hadn't been time to talk to a real estate agent—as usual, we were having far too much fun to fool with business—but we'd worry about that later. It was the kind of thing we were wont to put off. To tell you the truth, we might never have gotten around to selling it.

March was cold in our hollow. Don and I walked two miles every day with the dogs, but they were not leisurely walks. The cold made them brisk. We looked forward to soon shedding our coats. The dogs would shed theirs, too, and I'd be vacuuming twice a day.

Warmer weather was around the proverbial bend. Blooms were on the Bradford pears. The next-to-last Sunday in March we took a long drive along a picturesque Alabama road called the Rose Trail. We wore light jackets. We took a picnic. The dogwoods were just beginning to bloom but not quite yet in full glory. "They should be beautiful a week from now," I said. Don assured me we'd make the same drive in a week.

A year before, to mark our fifteenth year together, Don had built a raised bridge across the branch beside the farmhouse. For nearly a year we'd enjoyed it, sitting in the dappled sunshine that filtered through the sycamores. Somehow sitting below the farmhouse on that bridge changed our whole perspective of the property. I jokingly called it "the Bridge to Nowhere." But that wouldn't remain true long. Don kept clearing the land on the far side of the bridge, battling briars and spraying poison ivy. Soon the bridge went somewhere—to a pretty little clearing in the dark Mississippi woods.

As a Christmas gift for Don, two of our best Iuka friends, brothers Frank and Eddie Thomas, hand-stamped a plaque for the bridge. The metal stamp they used had belonged to their father. The sign said, in French, "*Le Nouveau Pont sur le ruisseau de Don Grierson, 2008.*" The New Bridge over the stream.

Don absolutely loved the gesture. He loved the brothers. He called them "Iuka's intelligentsia" and marveled at their musical abilities and far-reaching interests. "They are good company," he'd say. It was one of the few impractical Christmas gifts I'd ever seen him appreciate. He deplored the way people used Christmas to lavish one another with stuff they could not afford and that nobody needed. One year at a family function he had said polite thanks and placed his small stash of gifts, one by one, in a nest of wrapping paper beside him. When he opened a small red hand drill that Annie had found for him, he sighed: "Finally, something I can use."

But the little brass plaque touched him. The brothers Thomas had made it themselves. Don wanted to have a party that centered around affixing it to the bridge. I usually was the one who suggested parties, especially those with themes, and he'd go along. This time, he was the one who wanted to plan a party. But the weather remained spring nasty, and Don had a test scheduled to check for blockage in his carotids. We agreed it might be better to wait a couple of weeks on the party.

And we did.

## 22

# I'm So Lonesome I Could Cry

Pain is personal. When you rap your thumb with a hammer, nobody feels it but you. Nobody else cusses or cries. Grief is the same. The hammer hasn't hit anyone but you. People will bring you a cold rag to wrap your finger and say they are sorry you are hurting, but the endless throbbing doesn't go away when the sympathetic visitors do. It lasts. And lasts.

He was already dead when I found him. I know that now. I did not know it then. He was lying face down on the floor of our guest house, the one we'd built for extra space when we'd moved home to Mississippi from Georgia. The one with bookshelves that reached from floor to ceiling and were full of our books. He'd been using the little house for naps since surgery that was supposed to clean a blocked carotid artery. The surgery was four days earlier.

It was quiet in the guest house. I could turn off the phone in the little annex and go about my business in the main farmhouse. I could write or cook our meals or talk on the telephone without disturbing him. It was the same plan we'd used when Don had bypass surgery five years earlier. Once again, we had established a recovery routine.

The last day of the new routine was Sunday, March 29, 2009. We spent much of it watching television. We watched country music shows he'd recorded while away at the hospital. Don loved the *Midwest Country* and *Porter Wagoner Show* reruns on the RFD Network. He was fascinated with that network's trove of old tapes. I might be in another part of the house, and Don would shout excitedly, "Come quick. Do you want to see Bobby Bare? He's singing 'Streets of Baltimore.'"

We watched a movie we'd started but had not finished before his hospital stay. It was *Unforgiven* with Clint Eastwood. A cowboy movie with a message. A cowboy movie with a lot of shooting and death and an existentialist slant. *Shane* was Don's all-time favorite movie, and when *Unforgiven* was over he said, as he often did about movies, "It was good, but it was no *Shane*."

We ate lunch, ham sandwiches and soup, at the kitchen table. Our good friend Terry Martin stopped by for a minute to deliver Don's eyeglasses. Don had left them at the jeweler to be repaired. Don said he felt fine. He told Terry that. He told me that. He wasn't sore anymore as he had been the day after surgery. He took a shower, his first. He took the bandage off his strong neck. The stitches looked good, or as good as stitches can. He said he thought he'd feel like taking a long walk the next day.

Around four o'clock Don said he was going to take a nap so he'd feel rested enough to watch *60 Minutes* later. He nearly always watched *60 Minutes*. Between his voracious reading and a serious PBS habit, Don was the most informed man on the planet. I asked him if first he could chop up a fresh pineapple our friends Sue and Luke had brought him in a fruit basket. He did.

Don walked out the back door and took the path out to the little house, as I watched. I hollered after him. "I may take the dogs for a walk, but I won't be gone for long." I wasn't. Gone for long.

I wish I knew a few things. I wish I knew if he got up from bed to come back inside after about an hour of comfortable rest. Or, was he hurting and coming to look for me? Did he know, in a short millisecond of grim recognition, that he was about to die? Did he call out for me? Was I in the house or up the hill with the dogs? Would I have heard him from the house?

People who know lots more than I do about medical things tell me he did not suffer long. I know that is true. He wasn't even alone long. About an hour. But I know Don. And I know that if he realized, even for seconds, what was happening, he spent them worrying about me. And he suffered with the knowledge that I'd be half a soul without him. I would cope. He knew that. But I would never heal. Not ever. He would have known that, too.

We had Don's bridge party a week after he died. He would have approved. I think. Friends came from Seattle, from Berkeley, from Louisiana, from the Mississippi Coast. An old friend of Don's in Hattiesburg who suffers from lupus hired a driver to bring him up to the hills. Jeanette, who had never driven any farther than Baton Rouge, made the nine-hour trip up from Henderson with Johnelle, who is legally blind and cannot drive. Nearly a hundred people came. Chelsey was here, and I couldn't help but think of what she had said years ago when visiting us in Georgia. Don had just retired from teaching and was a young fifty-seven. We were tooling about Carrollton one day, Don at the wheel, when he missed a turn. Chelsey, who can be impatient, said to me in a conspiratorial whisper: "You know, I think since Don retired he's losing it."

He would have twelve more years without "losing it." His mind was as sharp on that last Sunday as it had ever been. He was reading *Narrow Dog to Carcassonne*, a funny travel book by the British writer Terry Darlington and *Judgment of Paris: California vs. France and the*

*Historic 1976 Paris Tasting That Revolutionized Wine* by George M. Taber, a book Jimmy had given him. And, as was his habit, he read every word in every *New Yorker* that arrived by mail weekly.

The acoustics in our hollow are good. Musician friends, including the Thomas boys, have told us that time and again. Sound reverberates between the hillsides that hold our house like two hands cupping water. We played Hank Williams music that afternoon of Don's bridge party. All Hank, all day. I wouldn't let anyone else touch the player. The music cried so we did not have to. The music spoke of heartbreak, predicted loneliness, forgave us our trespasses. It was sacred music in every sense.

We put a photograph of a smiling Don on an easel on the bridge; it did not match the music. It was taken the day he shot a big fish with a bow and arrow. It was the only time I remember that he asked to have his picture taken. "Go get the camera," he had said after reeling in his bass. In the photograph he is beaming.

Annie and I screwed the little brass plaque to the bridge before guests arrived. Everyone admired it. There was good food, but I did not eat. Except for cheese. For some reason, I ate cheese.

Don did not want a funeral service of any kind. Friends, however, wanted to say a few words. They almost insisted. I understood. It would have been wrong to say absolutely nothing about a man whose life said so much.

Annie told a story about a .38 snub-nose Smith and Wesson pistol her father Pete had won in a poker game and given her for protection. Don admired the gun, offered to buy it, and often would swap with Annie during target practice. Annie told Don to find her a replacement and she'd trade with him. Her gun was heavy anyway, she said. He bought her a gun, put it in a holster in the gun cabinet, but left

Pete's gun in the cabinet, too. She asked him why he didn't get it. "It's just fine where it is," he said.

About a year later Annie and Buba had company, Don was there, and the subject of the gun came up. "Annie made a whorehouse deal with that gun," Don said. "She had something I wanted. I bought it. I paid her for it. I got it. And she still has it."

Annie always figured Don, a patient man, had waited all that time, perhaps even contrived the whole deal, just to tell that story.

Tony Salmon of Seattle described how Don once fired him from the Natchez newspaper in such a gentle way that it didn't alter the friendship. They remained close friends. Tony said it bothered Don long after he himself had gotten over losing that reporter's job.

"Ironically, it was Don and the lead editor Murphy Givens who finally took me out for a drink at the Under the Hill Bar and, then, in the most good-natured manner possible, fired me," Tony wrote in a beautiful essay about Don after his death. "It was nothing personal, they said. Personally, they both liked me a lot. I just stunk as a news reporter. I couldn't even spell very well."

Larry Lepaule, who knew Don in the 1960s in Berkeley, came close to tears when he said a trip to the grocery with Don was an event. You didn't hang around Don long without hearing a quote worthy of needlepoint.

For my part, I read the poem "Dover Beach" and stumbled over the *let us be true to one another* part. We had been.

And, to quote more of Matthew Arnold's words, I knew for certain that day that this world *hath really neither joy, nor love, nor light. Nor certitude, nor peace, nor help for pain. . .*

Not anymore.

# 23

# Iron Eyes Cody and Calvinism

There was this list. It was on the window ledge near the end of the sofa Don occupied whenever he watched television. He had made such lists before. It was a list of things he meant to look up when our one computer, my work computer, was free and he felt like fooling with the internet. Those two planets rarely aligned.

After Don's death, I madly rushed about making work, staying busy so I could sleep at night without pills. Pills are not a good idea when you have dogs or babies. One day I found the "to look up" list on the ledge, and, without reading, quickly stuffed it in a folder with other bits of Don's handwriting. That seemed important. To save anything with his handwriting. I could pick out his printing or script from a thousand of such samples. He always used capital "E" and "A," even when the letters fell inside a word and there was no real need. He made the bottom line of his capital "L's" extremely long. He often retraced an "I."

I didn't read the list until months later. One day I remembered it and looked to see what he was last curious about. It read as follows: *Fred Allen, Doug Kershaw, Webb Pierce, Jim Reeves, Iron Eyes Cody, Jean Pruitt, Calvinism, Lusitania, Bernard Goetz, Leon Payne, Lisa Layne,*

*Willow Oak, Natchez Trace, Ambrose Bierce, A. Jackson, Cincinnati, Calzaghe, Harlan Howard.*

I wasn't surprised at the range of interest, everything from country music to Calvinism. This was a man who happily watched hours of *Beverly Hillbillies* reruns after rereading a Shakespearean tragedy for the umpteenth time. This was, or had been, a man who worked his way through college hanging Sheetrock, and had a master's in English and a passion for duck hunting. This was the man who had taught libel law at two universities and whose best friend was a Pascagoula factory worker. This was a man who could build a bridge, gig a frog, and write a poem.

I did not fall apart. Not at first. I was composed through the party, through the next several weeks, in fact. I wrote my column, never missing a single deadline, including the one due the Monday after Don's death on Sunday. I made speeches I had committed to make, including one to Alabama librarians the week after Don died. I wrote a few thank you notes, though that is not my long suit even in good times. I walked the dogs, who were grieving, too. Especially Mabel, the Lab, who looked for Don every time a truck came up the driveway. I drove down to Henderson with Mabel, who rushed from room to room barking. I think we both half expected to find him there. I tolerated visitors, though most folks had no clue what to say or what not to say. It never stops us from talking, does it? I finally understood why Don's conversation was so measured, so lean. He talked only when he really had something to say.

"What stage are you in?" one friend asked. "What stage are you on?" I felt like answering. It wasn't her fault. There is no right demeanor for death. There is no correct response to grief and the grieving.

We all think we'll be just like Jackie Kennedy was after JFK's assassination. A stylish, chin-up widow. One who looks good on camera. We will have dignity, and beauty, and good pearls. We will be gracious to well-meaning friends. We will be an example for our nieces and nephews and friends.

Bullshit.

More probably we will weep and wail and bitterly curse the fates. We will be mean to friends and, for some strange reason, tolerate enemies. We will quit brushing our teeth or caring what we eat. When we do eat, we'll look like an animal that suddenly remembers it is starving. We will sleep in our clothes and go to town in our pajamas. We will cut off our hair and leave our shoes untied. We won't remember where we put the lawn mower keys or the power bill or where we parked the car. We will back into utility poles and punish our bodies with alcohol that may well be a depressant but temporarily dulls the pain. We won't be Jackie Kennedy. We won't even recall who the hell she is.

People will start avoiding us. Who can blame them? Even the truest of friends can take only so much abuse, so much self-pity. We won't care. We will consort with strangers, the stranger the better. We will spend money we do not have and give away things we thought we could never live without.

Life turns not only upside down but inside out. Our guts are showing, our every nerve is exposed. It is not pretty. We are the Visible Woman, like the horse with its innards shining through clear plastic all those Christmases ago. The heart, can you see it? No, because it is gone.

We suspect this pain will never end. And it does not end. Not entirely. Not ever. But we learn to pretend, to utter the right sounds, to mouth the words that society expects at the appropriate moments. The words have no heft, no meaning, no passion. There is no passion left in the world anyhow. There is only the marking of time, and there's plenty of that.

We get out, which is a little better than staying home. Sometimes. We go to dinner parties and do not cry. We help arrange the flowers and set the table. We pretend things are interesting—conversation, trips, food, men. Nothing is.

We avoid the oddest things: The bent-can grocery store. The "men's" section of Belk's. The left side of the bed. Monogrammed linens. The Travel Channel. And, at all costs, the utility room where the Christmas decorations are stored.

Someone innocently asks, "What are you going to do for Christmas?" And we think but do not say aloud because that might cause alarm or, at the least, sound maudlin and that would never do: "Maybe I will die before Christmas and spare myself that."

# 24

# The Rest of My Life

The work saved me. I clung to it like flotsam in a boiling sea. It was the only solitary sport that I ever played, or was any good at. It felt natural to sit at my computer and type and type some more. For entire minutes, while writing, I could forget the godawful thing that had happened. I could forget that nothing really mattered anymore. Perhaps, if I set my sights low, I could care again about some small thing. I would type a word. One word. Then another.

I started to care about the words, then entire sentences. Eventually a paragraph would matter. When I'd quit work for the day, the meaningless hours came rushing, threatening to drown me, tsunami-style. So I would think about what I might write tomorrow and look forward to daylight. At night, when my eyes were tired from staring at a computer screen, I would talk on the phone, something I'd avoided in the past whenever possible. I almost liked it now. I needed it now. Talking on the phone proved you were still alive. I knew who rose at what hour. Whiskey Gray would be awake by 4 A.M., so he often got the first phone call. Bobbie Williams was up by 6. Anne Holtsford would be stirring by 7. Same drill at night. I knew who stayed up late, and that Californians were conveniently hours behind.

There is something almost liberating in having happen the worst that can happen. I no longer feared driving in heavy traffic. I drove to the Memphis airport the week after Don's party and didn't remember having done it. I no longer worried about snakes, once the bane of my country existence. Friends seeing to my dogs saw a rattlesnake in my backyard, and when they told me, it didn't bother me. I no longer cared about critics, either professional or personal. I wrote for myself again, the way I had in the Mississippi Delta where I'd been so happy. In another life. When column readers wrote to me and said I was an idiot, I didn't care. For the first time in a long career I honestly didn't care. My professional skin was so thick I could sit on nails and not wince. I ate anything I wanted. I ate cheese toast for breakfast, not high-fiber cereal. Fiber hadn't helped Don and he'd eaten tons of it. What was the point? The only thing that tasted good to me was cheese. Go figure.

You can write only so many hours a day, but those were the relatively good hours. They were the hours I was in control, when I could say anything I wanted and get paid a little for the privilege. The key phrase was "paid a little." Syndication dwindled. Newspapers were dying, too, same as Don. It looked to me like I might outlive everything I loved. I didn't care. I never wrote for money, anyhow, which makes me the idiot Samuel Johnson described when he said, "None but a blockhead writes for anything but money."

I did fear one thing: fall. I dreaded it with all my heart. Don loved fall. He loved the word "fall." He used to say that fall was the most aptly named season. He didn't like for people to use the prissier, multi-syllabic "autumn." Fall is, after all, when things fall: leaves, acorns that hit the house like mini-missiles, the temperature. He liked the simplicity and descriptiveness.

I felt fall move into the hollow early, in late August, as if to spite me. And I thought the coolness of the mornings and evenings might kill me. I had been right to fear it. The dogs grew livelier; Don would have said, "They know it's time to hunt." The sweet gums starting dropping their leaves, and the sumac began to turn red. I thought about the day Don looked up "sumac" in his worn dictionary and said you could pronounce it four ways: *Shoo-mac, Sue-mac. Sue-mock. Shoo-mock.* He cared about things like that.

Don should have been scouting out a dove field, cleaning his shotgun. He already would have had our wood laid up for the little Jøtul stove. We'd plan something special for the supper the first night cool enough for a fire. We'd eat in the kitchen and brag on the stove's efficiency.

Surely fall would kill me.

It didn't. Instead, despite everything, cooler weather made me start thinking about Christmas. Where I would spend it. Where I would put the tree this year. It wouldn't be Henderson. Not this year. The Henderson house was on the market, finally, just as we'd talked about. Not like we'd planned. All the potential buyers bothered me. They talked about cutting the pine trees. They talked about changing the wallpaper, pulling up the carpet in the bedrooms. I hated to hear about any change at the yellow house, though some of the changes I'd considered myself. What if someone painted the house another color? Don had chosen the yellow. He said your eye was drawn to the color yellow, and that his childhood home once had been the color of sunshine.

Johnelle, acting as real estate agent, reminded me time and again that selling the house was about money, you blockhead, not like putting a child up for adoption.

At first I couldn't remember if the Christmas ornaments that once were in the Henderson attic had been moved to Mississippi. I almost panicked. Then I remembered. They were in the utility shed out back, the one I'd been assiduously avoiding.

One woman who liked the Henderson house and wanted to buy it said she'd have to be settled in by Christmas. I understood.

We live from Christmas to Christmas. All of us. Whatever our beliefs, however ambivalent we are about celebrating, whether we'd rather spend it alone in a boat in the Louisiana swamp or a church pew in Peoria, Christmas is a demarcation, a way of keeping track. We remember our lives by our Christmases. What we gave. What we received. Who came to dinner. Who loved us. Where we were living, working, visiting.

Christmas is a calibration device, a way of measuring happiness, or unhappiness. It is a time line. When I was little, Christmas was magical, enchanted. Nothing compared with it. When I was young, Christmas was romantic, purple corduroy pants tied up with strings. When I was struggling, Christmas was respite, red beans and rice, a break in routine.

Now that I'm alone, Christmas is inevitable. But that inevitability is something, at least. Something to count on in a world where you cannot count on much. Christmas is coming, the goose is getting fat. You can bet on that.

Christmas is about children, many people insist. You hear that cloying sentiment time and again. And it can be. But only if you *have* children, or grandchildren, or extended family with bouncing babies they like to share. It can be about children. Chelsey and Ben are twenty-one. Maybe someday they will have children. Maybe not.

Christmas also can be about the old. It can be about wonderful grandparents like my Grannie, who picked up pecans to pay for the gifts she gave us, or Lucille, who cooked until she dropped. The old often figure into Christmas. They matter.

Those of us in between, this middle-aged slot in life when we slow but nobody notices, when we cry and nobody hears, we don't count so much at Christmas. Especially when we are without someone to say, "Are you depressed yet?" and care what we answer. We are in holiday purgatory, betwixt and between, middle-aged and middling, with beating hearts but slow pulses, thinking mostly of people who won't be at dinner, not those who will, but preparing dinner anyway.

Christmas is also about memories and misery and macabre stories that inevitably find their way into the slim issues of newspapers short-staffed for the holidays. Don used to tell a story from his Corpus Christi newspaper days. It involved a ditzy female receptionist whose main job was leading school kids on tours through the plant while wearing a pressman's hat made from a folded newspaper. One day, just before Thanksgiving, she rushed into the newsroom, excitedly waving a piece of paper with a phone number. "Who wants a nice Thanksgiving Day dog story?" she asked a room full of flinty-eyed reporters.

There are lots of those. Nice Thanksgiving Day dog stories. Heartwarming holiday fare, contrived fodder to make us feel good about the season. And then there are the real stories, the not so nice stories. They burst into the newsrooms, too. They find us.

I will have a tree this year nonetheless. I've decided. Surprise, surprise. Stop the presses. This year grieving is the reason for the season. I will march across Don's bridge and go into the woods and cut a cedar. The woods are thick with them, each one a dare. A double-dog dare.

I even looked inside the ornament box the other day. In it are the same old suspects: The crayon angel drawn by Sarah Crawford when she was five and her mother my best friend. The red sled Chelsey made from Popsicle sticks. A frame ornament holding a picture of Jimmy when he was about ten and got his first football uniform. A white porcelain rooster my friend Whiskey gave me one year. A fabric fleur-de-lis from the Louvre gift shop. A Santa Claus painted on a spoon by Sue Hall. A little ceramic bird in its blue ceramic birdhouse my sister Sheila made. A construction-paper mermaid painted by a Henderson girl named Libby with a Tiny Tim limp. A cartoonish duck hunter wildly waving his shotgun.

How could the holiday come and go if these ornaments remained in the box? If I don't hustle a tree from the red pickup to the porch, what would happen? Would the world stop spinning? I think it would. I'm not willing to risk it.

I am privileged to know the widow of the legendary, controversial, debonair journalist and novelist William Bradford Huie. He wrote *Three Lives for Mississippi* and *The Americanization of Emily*, plus other books and hundreds of provocative magazine articles. Martha Huie phoned one day to say she had heard about Don and was sorry. Taking full advantage of an empathetic ear, I started whining, listing things that were going wrong and breaking down at the farmhouse since Don was no longer around to fix them. I mentioned leaking pipes and limping cars and a litany of appliance woes. Martha was having none of it.

"I don't miss Bill so much when things go wrong," Martha wisely said. "I miss him when I see something beautiful, or something interesting happens. That's when I wish he were here."

She is right, of course. I wish most for Don when the dogs and I startle a covey of quails on our daily walk, or when a dozen wild turkeys are grazing the hay field, or when I get a note from one of his old friends who remembers something funny he said. I wish Don knew that National Public Radio had found its way to Henderson in the personal form of reporter Debbie Elliott, and that Jeanette's beautician wants to paint his portrait from my photograph that captured him and Mabel in the swamp. I wish he knew the *Green Queen* still has the little gas stove we moved there from his Smith Lake trailer, and that recent improvements to our old boat didn't ruin it. I wish he knew that the Henderson house is fetching a fair price and that I finished this book. I wish he knew Stan and Darlene bought his little sports car. All these would thrill him. Most of all, I wish he knew I'm all right, that friends are sticking by me, that Luke is weed-eating the steep bank and Tony is going to help load the U-Haul. I wish he knew I haven't crumpled completely but have soldiered on. He would like that.

Don went to see Annie less than a month before he died. It was Buba's birthday, and Don knew it would be a tough time for her. Anniversaries of any type are killers, or at least that's conventional wisdom. I now believe ordinary days may be much rougher than birthdays or holidays. We are distracted at Christmas, for instance. On a plain old Monday we have more time to think and must tackle the job of life alone.

I didn't go to Annie's that weekend. I had something else important to do. So important I can't remember what it was now. But I have imagined that evening at her home as a smorgasbord of memories and stories and tears, a "letting," if you will, of emotion and love. After Don's death just days later, Annie told me about a little about the gathering. Everyone stayed up too late and talked a lot about Buba, his quiet and good life. As he was leaving her house the morning after the birthday "celebration," Don looked at Annie and he said in his quiet, even drawl: "There's nothing for us to do, Annie, but keep moving forward."

Keep moving forward. Three words to remember when you want to forget.

∾